I0816413

First published in 2025 by Hungry Tomato Ltd
F15, Old Bakery Studios, Blewetts Wharf,
Malpas Road, Truro, Cornwall, TR1 1QH, UK.

Thanks to our creative team:
Edited by Jenny Rowan
Book design by Meg Holbrook
Dinosaur consultant: Dr Charlotte Bird

Information in this book is up to date as of the time of writing.

Beetle Books is an imprint of Hungry Tomato.

A CIP catalog record for this book is available from the British Library.

BEETLE BOOKS

ISBN: 9781835690925 (hard cover)
ISBN: 9781835697306 (soft cover)

Printed and bound in China

Discover more at
www.hungrytomato.com

FSC www.fsc.org MIX Paper | Supporting responsible forestry FSC® C158492

DINOSAURS

An illustrated guide to 100 amazing dinosaurs!

By Rosie Rowntree & Eliza Jeffery
Illustrated by Marina Halak

CONTENTS

Deadly Dinosaurs

Battle-Ready Dinosaurs

Record-Breaking Dinosaurs

Funky-Featured Dinosaurs

Words in **bold** can be found in the glossary.

THE WORLD OF DINOSAURS

Get ready to explore the wonderful world of dinosaurs! From the tiny Yanornis to the giant Patagotitan, there are so many different types of dinosaurs to discover.

WHAT WERE THE DINOSAURS?

Dinosaurs were a group of **reptiles** that lived on Earth millions upon millions of years ago. They ranged in size from the bird-sized Confuciusornis (page 55) to the house-sized Brachiosaurus (page 46). The word "dinosaur" comes from two Greek words meaning "terrible" and "lizard".

WHEN DID THE DINOSAURS LIVE?

Dinosaurs lived on Earth for almost 180 million years. But they didn't all live at the same time! Some were around later than others. Scientists think that the earliest dinosaurs first appeared over 245 million years ago, while the last roamed the Earth 66 million years ago.

WHAT HAPPENED TO THE DINOSAURS?

66 million years ago, a large **asteroid** hit Earth at incredibly high speed. It caused a lot of fires and sent huge waves crashing across the land. Dust from the asteroid affected the weather and reduced the amount of food that the dinosaurs had to eat.

This made most dinosaurs become **extinct** – except for those that could fly, which survived and developed into the birds that we are familiar with today!

Dinosaurs like Yi Qi (page 58) can teach us a lot about the history of birds.

An almost complete skeleton of T.rex (page 13) has been found by scientists!

WHAT ARE FOSSILS?

Fossils are the remains of animals and plants that have been preserved for millions of years. They have been found on all seven of Earth's **continents**! Fossils of a dinosaur's entire **skeleton** are very rare. But even if they are found in bits and pieces, fossils allow scientists to learn a lot about the dinosaurs and their lives!

TYPES OF DINOSAURS

Scientists have arranged the dinosaurs into different categories based on things that they had in common, like their size or the way that they walked.

THEROPODS

Theropods all walked on two legs. Smaller theropods often had feathers, while larger ones were some of the biggest meat-eaters ever!

PACHYCEPHALOSAURS

These dinosaurs also walked on two legs. They are best known, however, for having very tough skulls!

CERATOPSIANS

These plant-eating dinosaurs had large eye-catching frills on their heads that could be used for protection. Their frills also helped them to keep warm in cold weather.

ORNITHOPODS

Ornithopods included several dinosaurs with duck-like beaks and crests on their heads. They were all plant-eaters rather than meat-eaters.

SAUROPODS

Sauropods included some of the largest dinosaurs to ever walk the Earth! They are easy to identify because they all had very long necks and tails, with incredibly small heads in comparison.

STEGOSAURS

Stegosaurs walked on four legs. Their most iconic features are the incredibly tough plates that ran across their backs and provided them with protection.

ANKYLOSAURS

Like stegosaurs, ankylosaurs had protective plates across their bodies. Ankylosaurs, however, had much shorter legs and often had tails that were shaped like clubs.

PTEROSAURS

These reptiles were close cousins of the dinosaurs and were the first animals after insects to develop the ability to fly. The very biggest had a similar wingspan to a small plane!

DEADLY DINOSAURS

The most ferocious dinosaurs of all were those with incredible features that helped them track and catch prey. Some had terribly sharp teeth and claws for grabbing onto their victims. Others were deadly because they were speedy or stealthy, had super keen senses, or hunted as a pack. The dinosaurs in this chapter were not to be messed with!

Tyrannosaurus rex

The most famous dinosaur of all, Tyrannosaurus rex was also one of the biggest land **predators** to have ever walked on Earth! It had huge teeth – bigger than any other dinosaur – which were perfect for crunching through skin and bone.

PRONUNCIATION: tie-RAN-oh-SORE-us rex

DIET: Carnivore

TIME PERIOD: Late **Cretaceous**

SIZE	4 of 5
SPEED	3 of 5
DEADLY RATING	5 of 5

Deinonychus

Deinonychus's name means "terrible claw" – it's easy to see why! This dinosaur had an extra large claw on each foot, which it would have used to latch onto and pin its **prey** against the ground. It is also likely that it had feathers!

PRONUNCIATION: dye-NON-ick-us

DIET: Carnivore

TIME PERIOD: Early Cretaceous

SIZE

SPEED

DEADLY RATING

Spinosaurus

Spinosaurus is the largest meat-eating animal to ever live! It hunted in and around water, using its long snout to catch any unsuspecting fish or other marine creatures. Its nostrils were far back on its head, which meant it could breathe even when partly underwater.

PRONUNCIATION: SPINE-oh-SORE-us

DIET: Carnivore

TIME PERIOD: Late Cretaceous

SIZE

SPEED

DEADLY RATING

Allosaurus

Allosaurus was one of the fiercest dinosaurs of its time! Nothing was safe from this large predator, even other dinosaurs! With its backward-curving teeth, once Allosaurus gripped its prey there was no way to escape.

PRONUNCIATION: AL-oh-sore-us

DIET: Carnivore

TIME PERIOD: Late **Jurassic**

SIZE

SPEED

DEADLY RATING

Compsognathus

Compsognathus may have been no bigger than a chicken, but what it lacked in size it made up for in speed! Its strong back legs propelled it across the ground incredibly quickly when chasing prey.

PRONUNCIATION: komp-sog-NATH-us

DIET: Carnivore

TIME PERIOD: Late Jurassic

SIZE

SPEED

DEADLY RATING

Coelophysis

Coelophysis was one of the earliest known carnivorous dinosaurs. It had **hollow** bones that made it very light on its feet, and forward-facing eyes that gave it excellent vision. This, mixed with its sharp claws and teeth, made it a very deadly predator.

PRONUNCIATION: seel-OH-fie-sis

DIET: Carnivore

TIME PERIOD: Late **Triassic**

SIZE

SPEED

DEADLY RATING

Carcharodontosaurus

This dinosaur had many similarities to Tyrannosaurus rex (page 13). It was as tall as a double-decker bus with small arms and as many as 60 teeth. But Carcharodontosaurus and T.rex lived in different parts of the world at different times, so these two giants would never have met.

PRONUNCIATION: kar-KAR-o-don-toe-sore-us

DIET: Carnivore

TIME PERIOD: Late Cretaceous

SIZE

SPEED

DEADLY RATING

Helicoprion

This shark-like creature had a **unique** spiral-shaped lower jaw called a "whorl"! It would have acted like a saw, allowing Helicoprion to eat both hard- and soft-bodied prey.

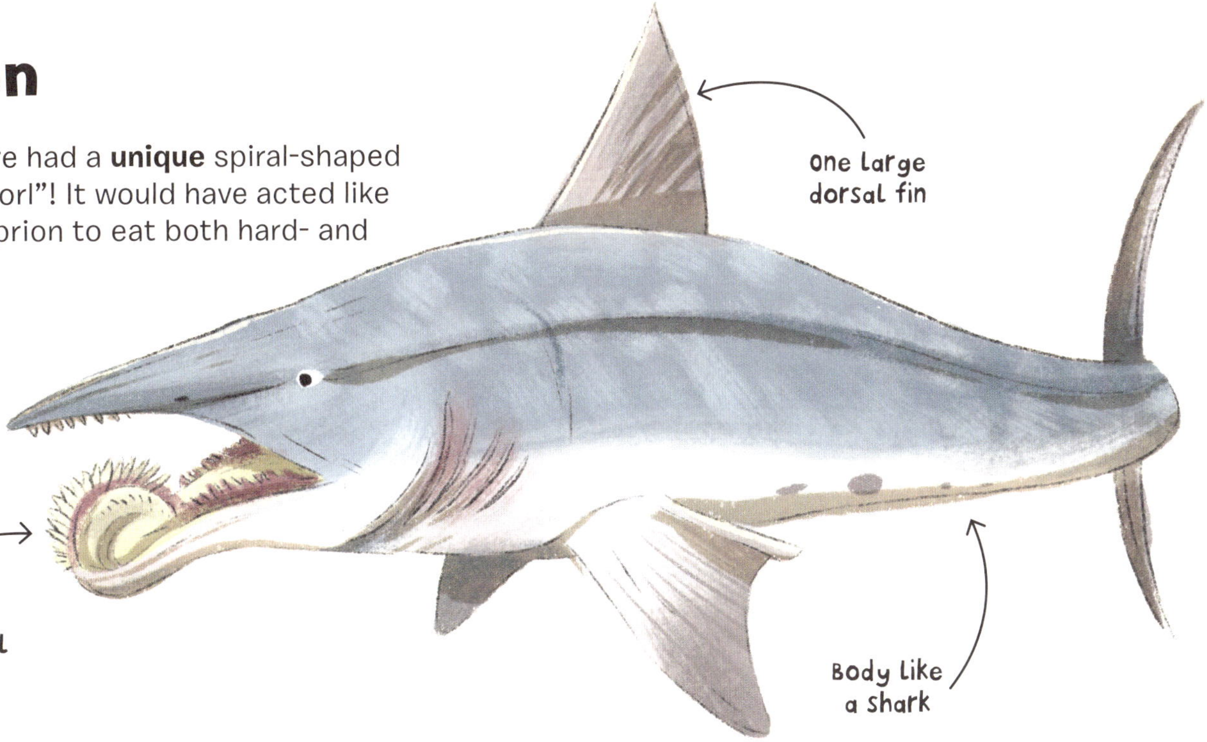

One large dorsal fin

Spiral-shaped whorl

Body like a shark

PRONUNCIATION: hel-ee-KO-pree-on

DIET: Carnivore

TIME PERIOD: Early **Permian**

SIZE

SPEED

DEADLY RATING

Microraptor

Microraptor is one of the smallest dinosaurs ever found! Despite having four wings, it isn't certain if it could fly properly. Instead, it likely jumped from branches high up in the trees and glided through the air in search of insects, small **mammals**, and fish to eat.

PRONUNCIATION: MIKE-roe-rap-tor

DIET: Carnivore

TIME PERIOD: Early Cretaceous

SIZE

SPEED

DEADLY RATING

worked in teams

Stenonychosaurus

Fast and with great vision, Stenonychosaurus was a very smart dinosaur. It had the largest brain relative to its size of any dinosaur, and it is thought that it hunted in groups to take down much larger prey! For many years scientists thought that its fossils were from another dinosaur called Troodon. But they now think that most of those fossils did in fact belong to Stenonychosaurus!

Large eyes

Long fingers

Slender legs

PRONUNCIATION: sten-oh-NYE-ko-sore-us

DIET: Omnivore

TIME PERIOD: Late Cretaceous

SIZE

SPEED

DEADLY RATING

Velociraptor

Even though it was covered in feathers, Velociraptor's short arms meant it couldn't actually fly! Instead, the feathers were likely used to shield itself or its nests from the cold. Light and **agile**, Velociraptor chased after its prey and used its long claws to pin them down.

Long, stiff tail

Thick arm feathers

Sharp claws on each foot

PRONUNCIATION: vel-OSS-i-rap-tor	**SIZE** ●●○○○
DIET: Carnivore	**SPEED** ●●●●○
TIME PERIOD: Late Cretaceous	**DEADLY RATING** ●●●○○

Liopleurodon

These giant marine reptiles likely had no predators! They were at the top of the **food chain** and used their large flippers to push themselves through the water in search of large fish and other marine reptiles to feast on.

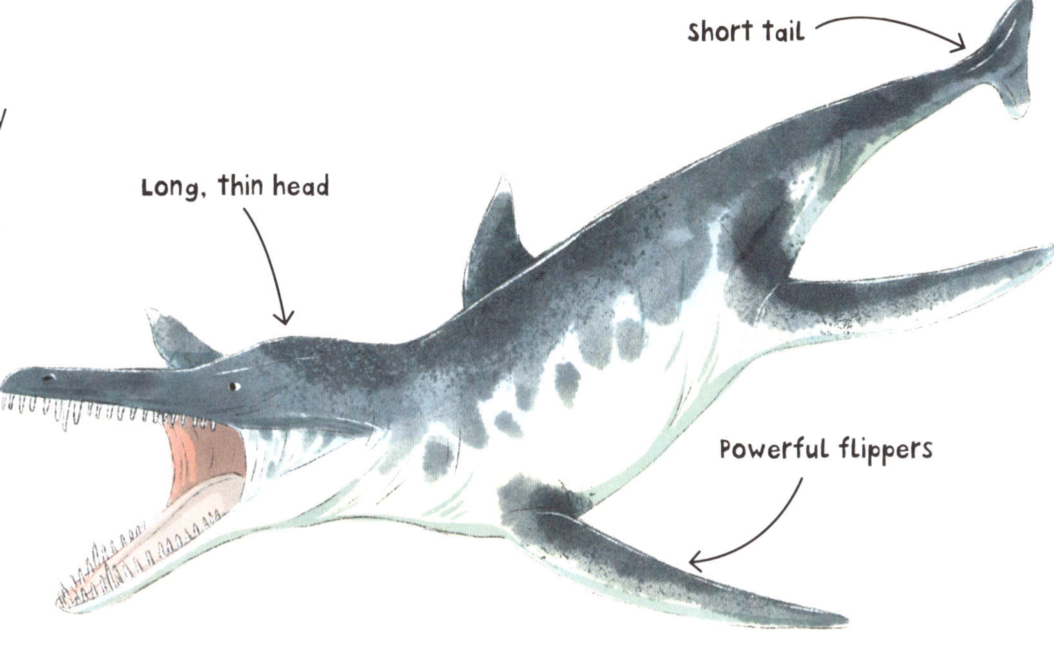

PRONUNCIATION: lee-oh-PLUR-oh-don	**SIZE**
DIET: Omnivore	**SPEED**
TIME PERIOD: Mid to late Jurassic	**DEADLY RATING**

Albertosaurus

This dinosaur was large and powerful. It is often compared to Tyrannosaurus rex (page 13) and shares many similarities, including its short arms, strong bite, and large skull. It is possible that they hunted in groups – how terrifying!

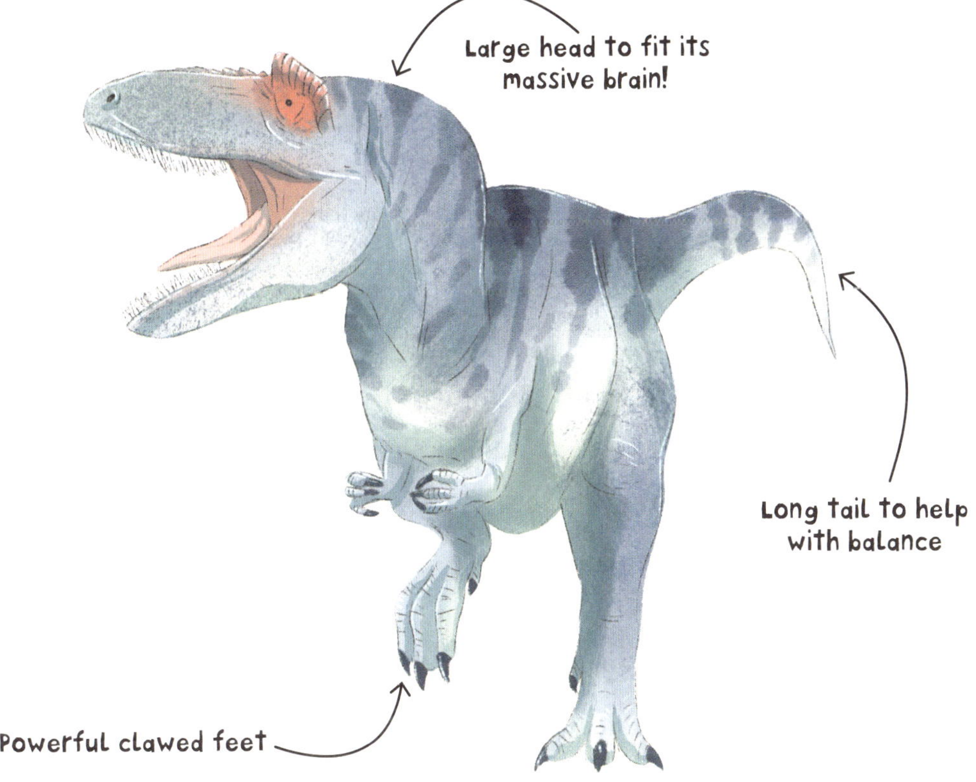

PRONUNCIATION: al-BERT-oh-SORE-russ	**SIZE**	   
DIET: Carnivore	**SPEED**	
TIME PERIOD: Late Cretaceous	**DEADLY RATING**	  

Dakotaraptor

Dakotaraptor is one of the largest feathered theropods ever found! But despite its size and weight, it was still very agile, fast, and good at jumping. This made it a very intimidating predator.

Had feathers but was too heavy to fly!

Huge claws on both its arms and feet

PRONUNCIATION: da-KOH-ta-rap-tor	**SIZE**
DIET: Carnivore	**SPEED** 
TIME PERIOD: Cretaceous	**DEADLY RATING**

Ceratosaurus

Ceratosaurus had a sharp horn on its head and small pieces of bony armor/armour running along its back. It seems that this was quite a rare dinosaur, and a lot about it is still a mystery. Scientists still don't know what its horn was actually used for!

PRONUNCIATION: sir-AT-oh-SORE-us	**SIZE**    
DIET: Carnivore	**SPEED** 
TIME PERIOD: Late Jurassic	**DEADLY RATING**   

Giganotosaurus

As its name suggests, Giganotosaurus was gigantic! Not only was it very tall, it was also very fast and preyed on other large dinosaurs. There is also evidence of it living in family groups.

PRONUNCIATION: gig-an-OH-toe-SORE-us

DIET: Carnivore

TIME PERIOD: Early Cretaceous

SIZE

SPEED

DEADLY RATING

Plesiosaurus

These marine reptiles had four large flippers. It is believed that the front pair were used for pushing Plesiosaurus through the water, while the back pair were to help with direction. They moved up and down rather than from side to side, making Plesiousaurus's style of swimming very unusual!

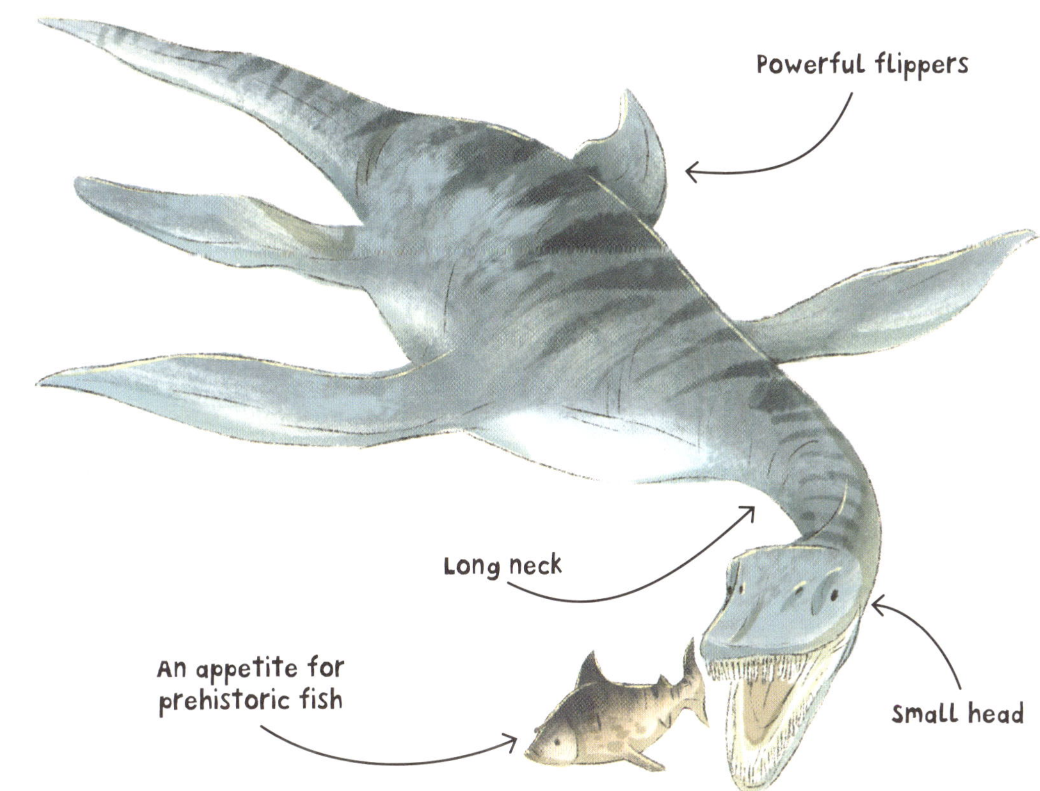

PRONUNCIATION: PLE-see-oh-SORE-us

DIET: Carnivore

TIME PERIOD: Jurassic

SIZE

SPEED

DEADLY RATING

Rugops

Rugops is a very mysterious dinosaur to science. The only fossil ever found of it is a skull! It was likely that it had scales on its head and possibly the rest of its body. It may also have been a **scavenger**, picking up the scraps left behind by other hunters.

PRONUNCIATION: ROO-gops

DIET: Carnivore

TIME PERIOD: Late Cretacious

SIZE

SPEED

DEADLY RATING

Dilophosaurus

Dilophosaurus featured two distinctive crests on the top of its head, made from the same material as human hair and nails! Despite its large size, this dinosaur is thought to have been fast, and had sharp claws that it used to catch and hold onto its prey.

PRONUNCIATION: die-LOAF-oh-sore-us

DIET: Carnivore

TIME PERIOD: Early Jurassic

SIZE

SPEED

DEADLY RATING

Baryonyx

This dinosaur's head looked a lot like a crocodile's! Its teeth were cone-shaped rather than blade-shaped, and it had an amazingly big claw at the end of each arm that it used to hook slippery fish out of the water.

PRONUNCIATION: bah-ree-ON-icks	SIZE
DIET: Carnivore	SPEED
TIME PERIOD: Early Cretaceous	DEADLY RATING

Carnotaurus

Carnotaurus was a fearsome-looking dinosaur with two prominent horns on its head. Rather than being used for hunting prey, these horns were likely used for ramming or shoving one another. But despite its intimidating face, Carnotaurus had tiny arms!

PRONUNCIATION: kar-noh-TORE-us	SIZE	   
DIET: Carnivore	SPEED	  
TIME PERIOD: Late Cretaceous	DEADLY RATING	  

Majungasaurus

Majungasaurus grew a new set of teeth every two months! This is the fastest growth rate of any meat-eating dinosaur. This suggests it didn't just eat the meat of its prey, but it chomped on their bones too!

PRONUNCIATION: mah-joon-gah-SORE-us

DIET: Carnivore

TIME PERIOD: Late Cretaceous

SIZE	
SPEED	
DEADLY RATING	

Sinornithosaurus

Even though it had feathers like a modern-day bird, this dinosaur couldn't fly. It was, however, good at leaping. Its long tail helped it to keep its balance as it jumped from spot to spot either to chase prey or to escape from predators.

PRONUNCIATION: sine-or-NITH-oh-SORE-us

DIET: Carnivore

TIME PERIOD: Early Cretaceous

SIZE	  
SPEED	  
DEADLY RATING	 

Dracorex

Even though its name means “dragon king”, Dracorex was very much a dinosaur. Its skull featured multiple horns and spikes. Because it was a **herbivore**, these wouldn’t have been used to catch prey. Instead, they would have been used to help Dracorex defend itself from predators.

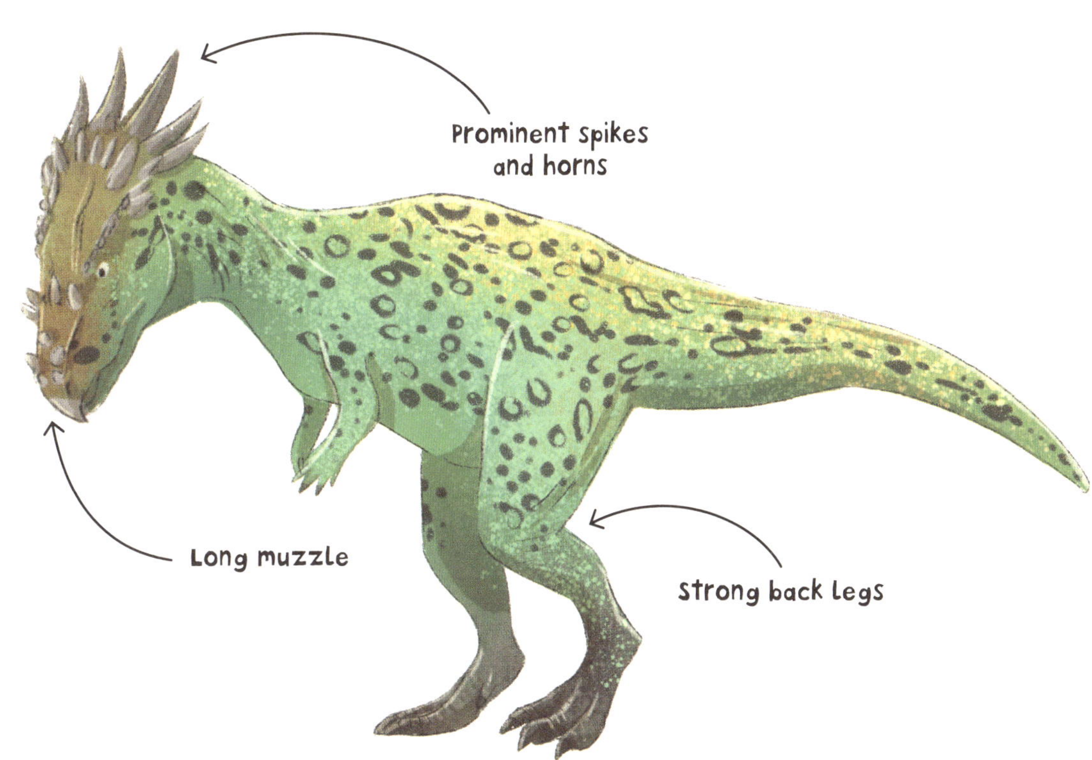

PRONUNCIATION: dray-KO-rex

DIET: Herbivore

TIME PERIOD: Late Cretaceous

SIZE

SPEED

DEADLY RATING

Mapusaurus

Mapusaurus was one of the largest meat-eating dinosaurs ever. Scientists have found evidence that suggests it hunted and lived in groups, meaning it would have been able to take on and overpower even the very biggest plant-eating dinosaurs.

PRONUNCIATION: mah-puh-SORE-us

DIET: Carnivore

TIME PERIOD: Late Cretaceous

SIZE  

SPEED 

DEADLY RATING   

BATTLE-READY DINOSAURS

Some dinosaurs didn't just survive – they had to fight for their lives! With fearsome features like sharp claws, tough skulls, and powerful tails, these creatures had all the tools they needed to fight off attackers and take down prey. Whether striking out alone or finding safety in numbers, the dinosaurs in this chapter were built for battle!

Weighed as much as an elephant

Therizinosaurus

This huge dinosaur had the longest claws of any animal in history! They were mainly used for hooking onto **vegetation** and pulling it towards its mouth to munch on. But they could also have been used for slashing at any predator bold enough to try and take it on.

PRONUNCIATION: THER-ih-zine-oh-SORE-us

DIET: Herbivore

TIME PERIOD: Late Cretaceous

SIZE

SPEED

DEADLY RATING

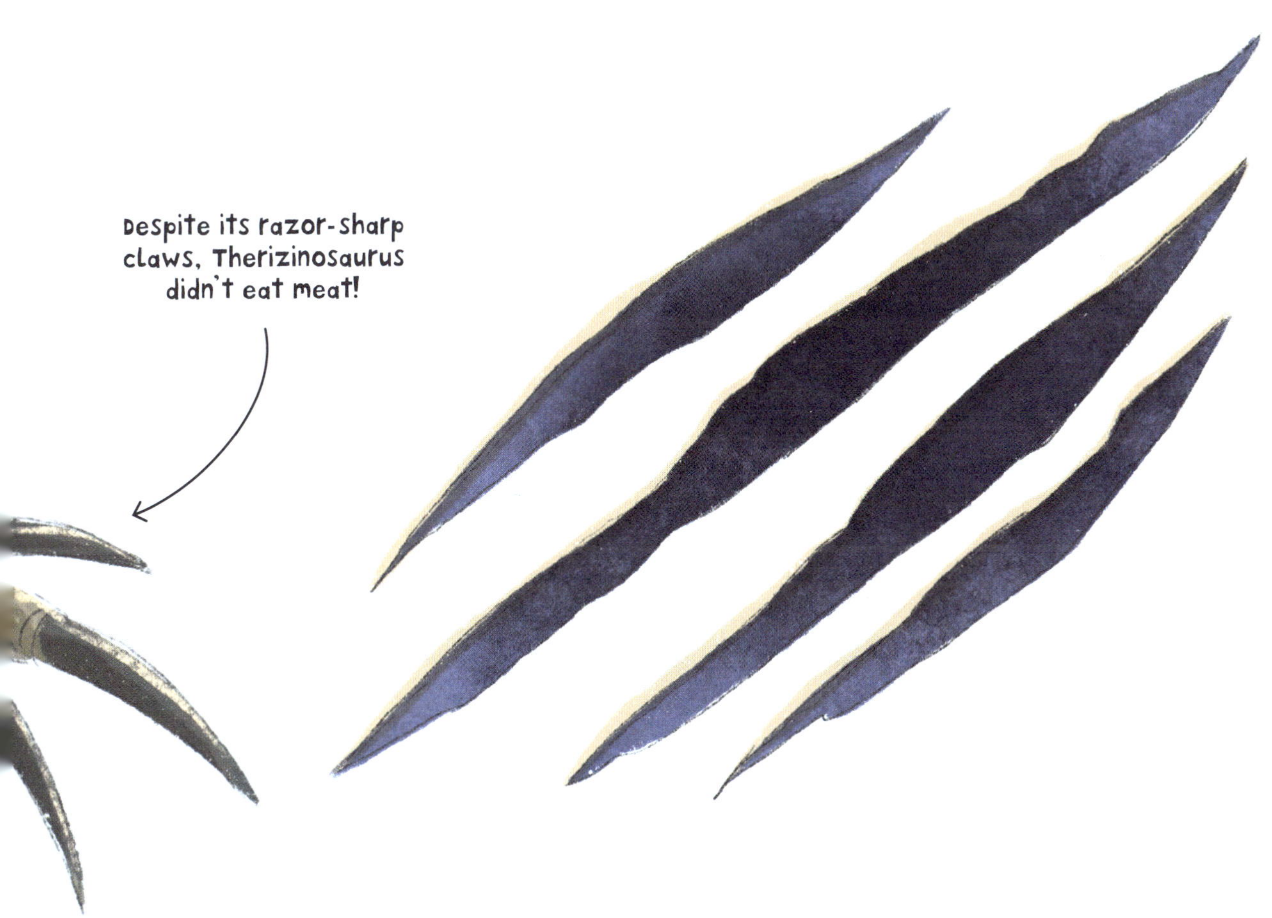

Pachycephalosaurus

Despite being a plant-eater rather than a meat-eater, this dinosaur wasn't afraid of a fight! Pachycephalosaurus had a distinctive dome-shaped head, which it used for ramming into its opponents. Its thick skull helped to protect its brain while it did so.

PRONUNCIATION: pack-ee-KEF-al-oh-sore-us

DIET: Herbivore

TIME PERIOD: Late Cretaceous

	Rating (out of 5)
SIZE	2
SPEED	3
DEADLY RATING	2

Its name means 'thick-headed lizard'

Fought to defend its food and land

Ankylosaurus

Ankylosaurus was the tank of the dinosaur world! Its body was covered in armor/armour and spikes, and it had a thick tail like a club. It would have swung this tail like a weapon, fending off predators and fighting for territory.

PRONUNCIATION: an-KEE-low-sore-us

DIET: Herbivore

TIME PERIOD: Late Cretaceous

SIZE

SPEED

DEADLY RATING

Achelousaurus

This dinosaur was a cousin of Triceratops (page 32)! It had a distinctive frill on its head which it used to defend itself and to keep its brain cool in warm weather! Two horns at the top of the frill would have been used to fight off other dinosaurs.

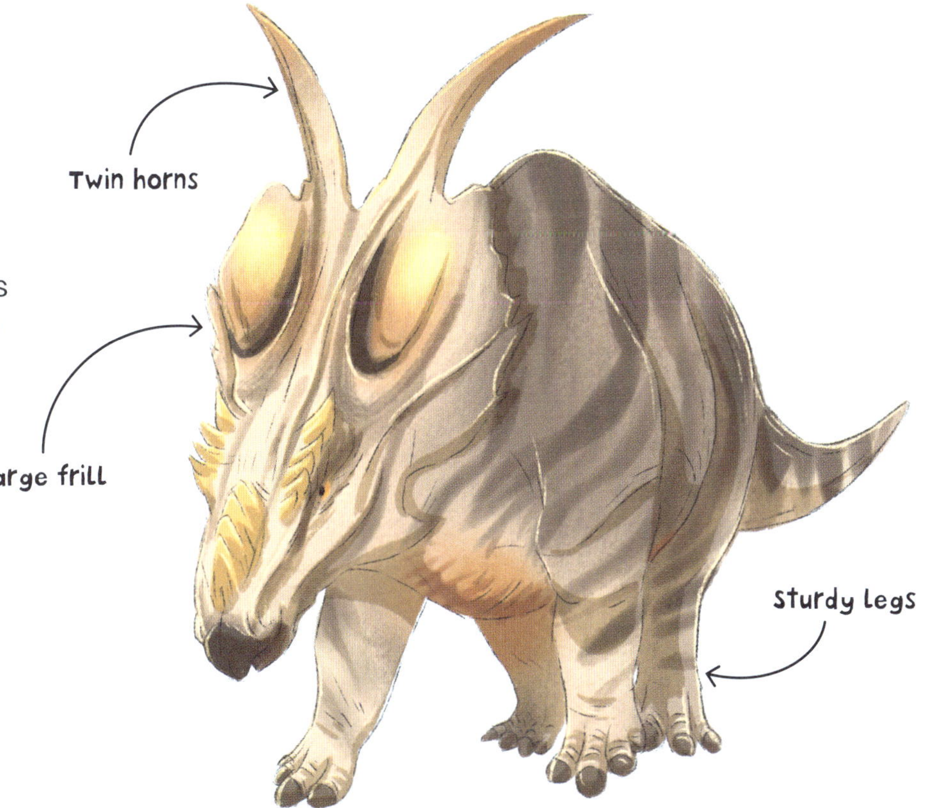

PRONUNCIATION: ah-KEL-oo-SORE-us

DIET: Herbivore

TIME PERIOD: Late Cretaceous

SIZE

SPEED

DEADLY RATING

Triceratops

The intimidating-looking Triceratops had a name that means "three-horned face". Two large horns on its head and a smaller one on its nose - as well as the frill around its neck - made it one of the most easily identifiable dinosaurs of all!

Iconic frill

Large skull

Mouth like a beak

PRONUNCIATION: tri-SER-a-tops

DIET: Herbivore

TIME PERIOD: Late Cretaceous

SIZE

SPEED

DEADLY RATING

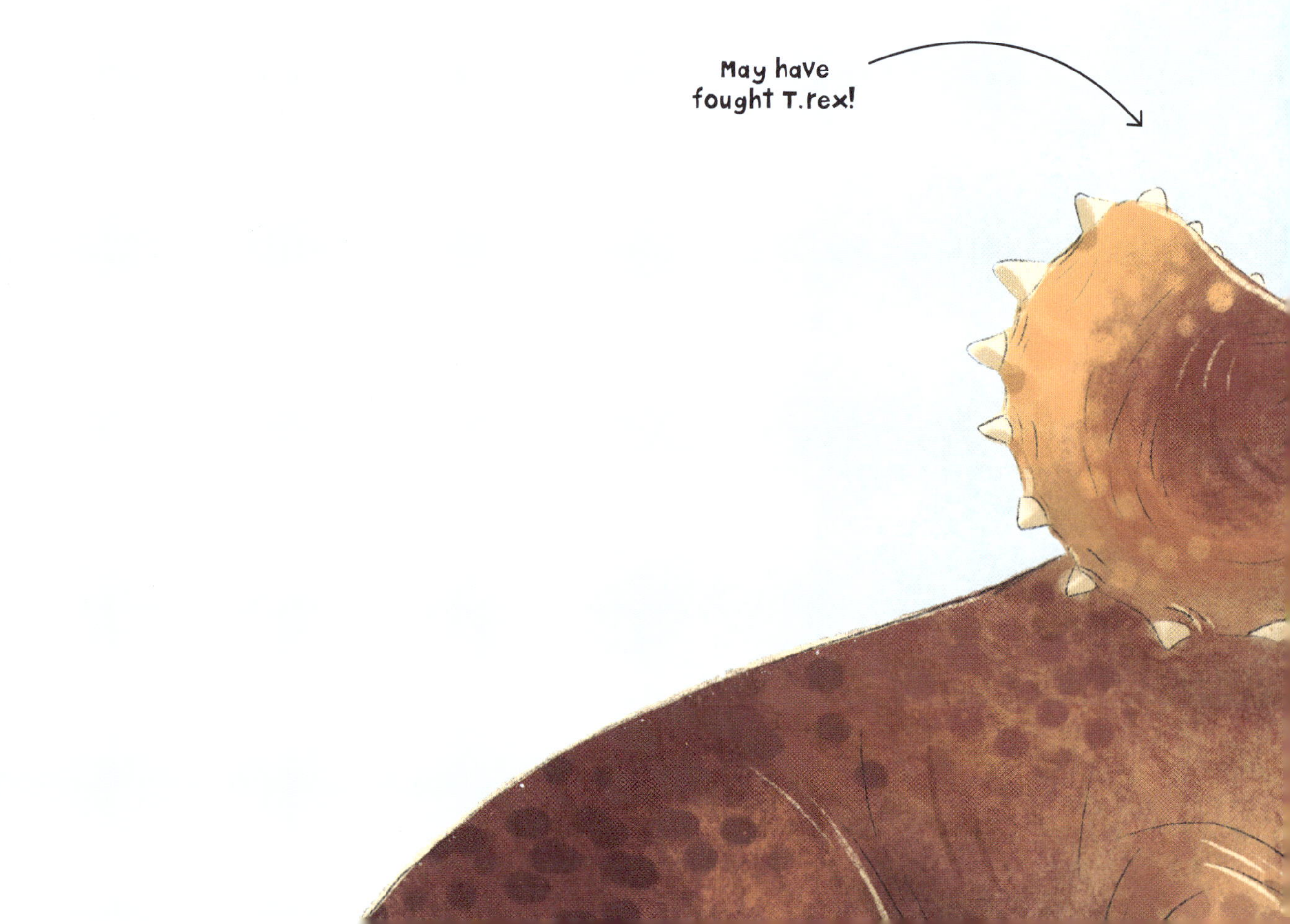

Large horns to help
protect itself
from predators

Euoplocephalus

Heavy and sturdy, Euoplocephalus was well protected by the plating and spikes that covered its back. It even had ridges on its face to help shield its eyelids! Most notable of all was its large club tail that could be swung with immense force to fight off larger dinosaurs.

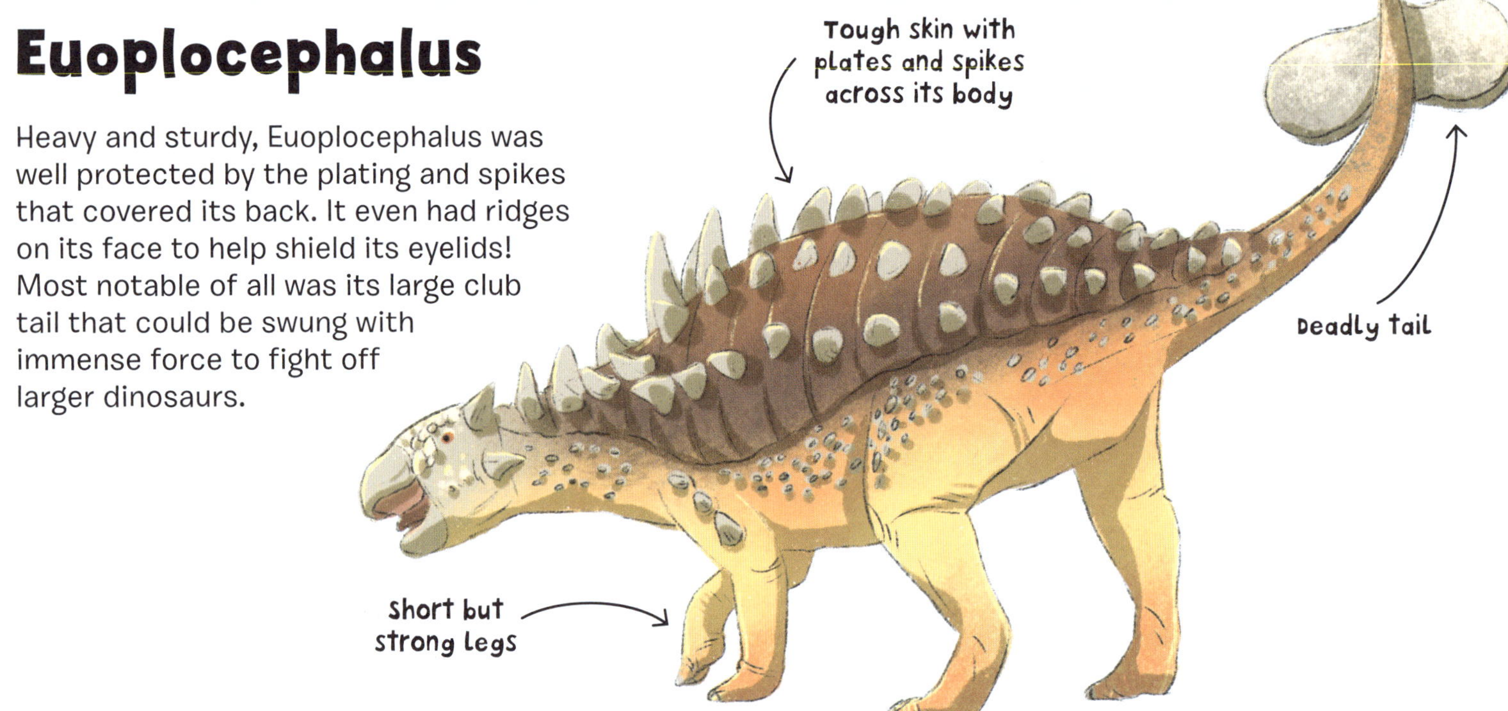

PRONUNCIATION: you-OH-plo-kef-ah-luss

DIET: Herbivore

TIME PERIOD: Late Cretaceous

SIZE

SPEED

DEADLY RATING

Cryolophosaurus

Cryolophosaurus was the first meat-eating dinosaur discovered in what is now Antarctica. It was the largest predator there at the time, and is best identified by the distinctive crest on its head.

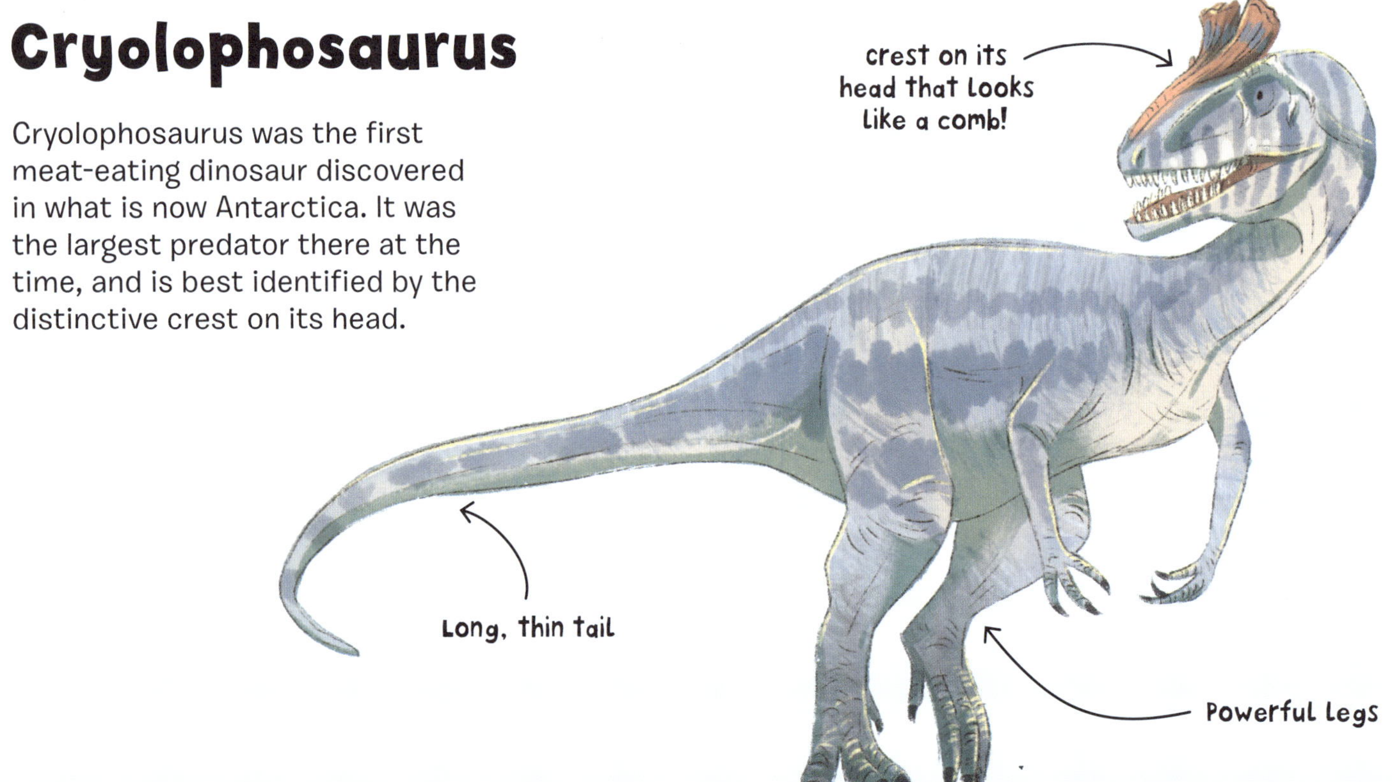

PRONUNCIATION: cry-oh-LOAF-oh-sore-us

DIET: Carnivore

TIME PERIOD: Early Jurassic

SIZE

SPEED

DEADLY RATING

Diabloceratops

Diabloceratops's appearance is certainly impressive! Not only did it have two large horns on its head, it had two even larger, curved ones on top of its frill. One look at it would have been enough to make any dinosaur think twice about attacking!

PRONUNCIATION: dee-AH-blow-ser-a-tops

DIET: Herbivore

TIME PERIOD: Late Cretaceous

SIZE

SPEED

DEADLY RATING

Stygimoloch

This dinosaur's thick skull and long horns, combined with its speed and agility, made it a tough opponent. That's despite its relatively small size! Some scientists, however, believe that it is actually a young Pachycephalosaurus (page 30) rather than a **species** of its own!

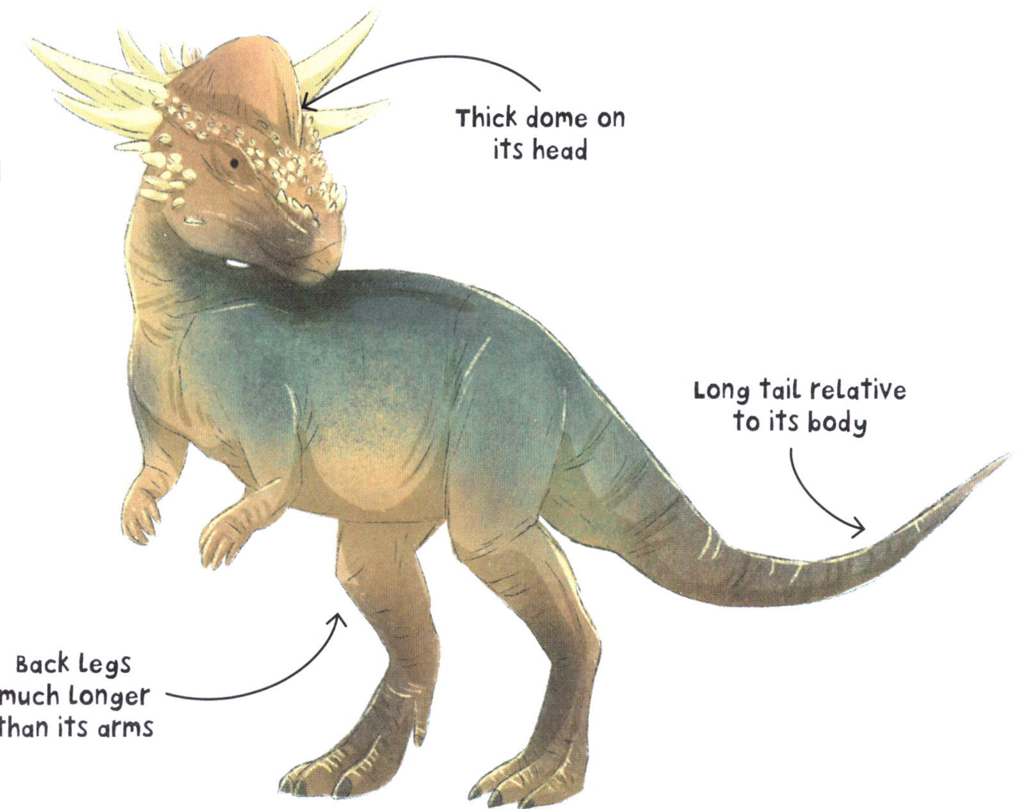

PRONUNCIATION: STIJ-ee-mol-ok

DIET: Herbivore

TIME PERIOD: Late Cretaceous

SIZE

SPEED

DEADLY RATING

Pentaceratops

Pentaceratops belonged to the same family of dinosaurs as Triceratops (page 32) and has a name that means 'five-horned face'. It did indeed have five horns: one on its nose, two on top of its head, and two on the side of its head.

PRONUNCIATION: penta-ah-KER-ah-tops

DIET: Herbivore

TIME PERIOD: Late Cretaceous

SIZE

SPEED

DEADLY RATING

Jakapil

The tiny Jakapil is thought to have been no bigger than a cat! But despite its incredibly small size, it wasn't helpless. Jakapil was covered in tough skin from its neck to its tail and had multiple spikes that helped to protect it.

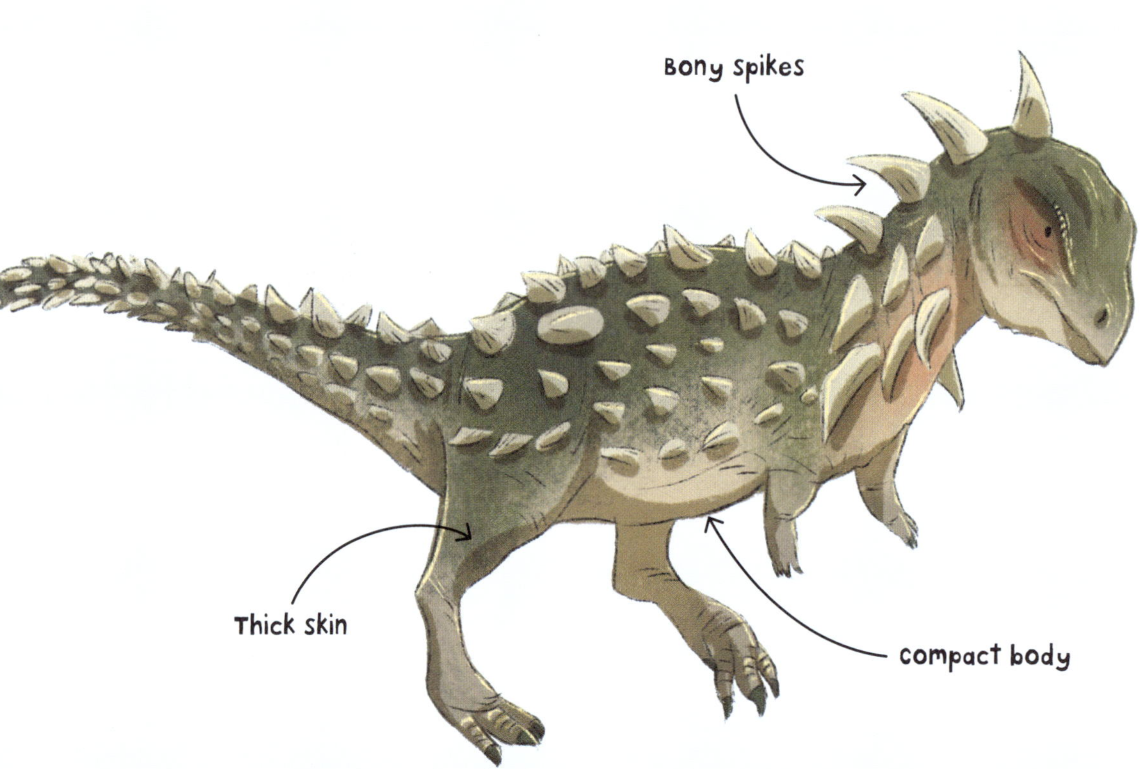

PRONUNCIATION: jah-KAH-pil

DIET: Herbivore

TIME PERIOD: Late Cretaceous

SIZE

SPEED

DEADLY RATING

Stegoceras

Stegoceras was part of the same group of dinosaurs as Pachycephalosaurus (page 30) and shared a similar dome-shaped head. Stegoceras was the smallest member of this group and had a very good sense of smell.

PRONUNCIATION: ste-GO-ser-as

DIET: Herbivore

TIME PERIOD: Late Cretaceous

SIZE

SPEED

DEADLY RATING

Chasmosaurus

Chasmosaurus had smaller horns than other similar dinosaurs but had an incredibly large frill that was the shape of a rectangle. It would have been used to protect Chasmosaurus's neck or to attract a **mate**.

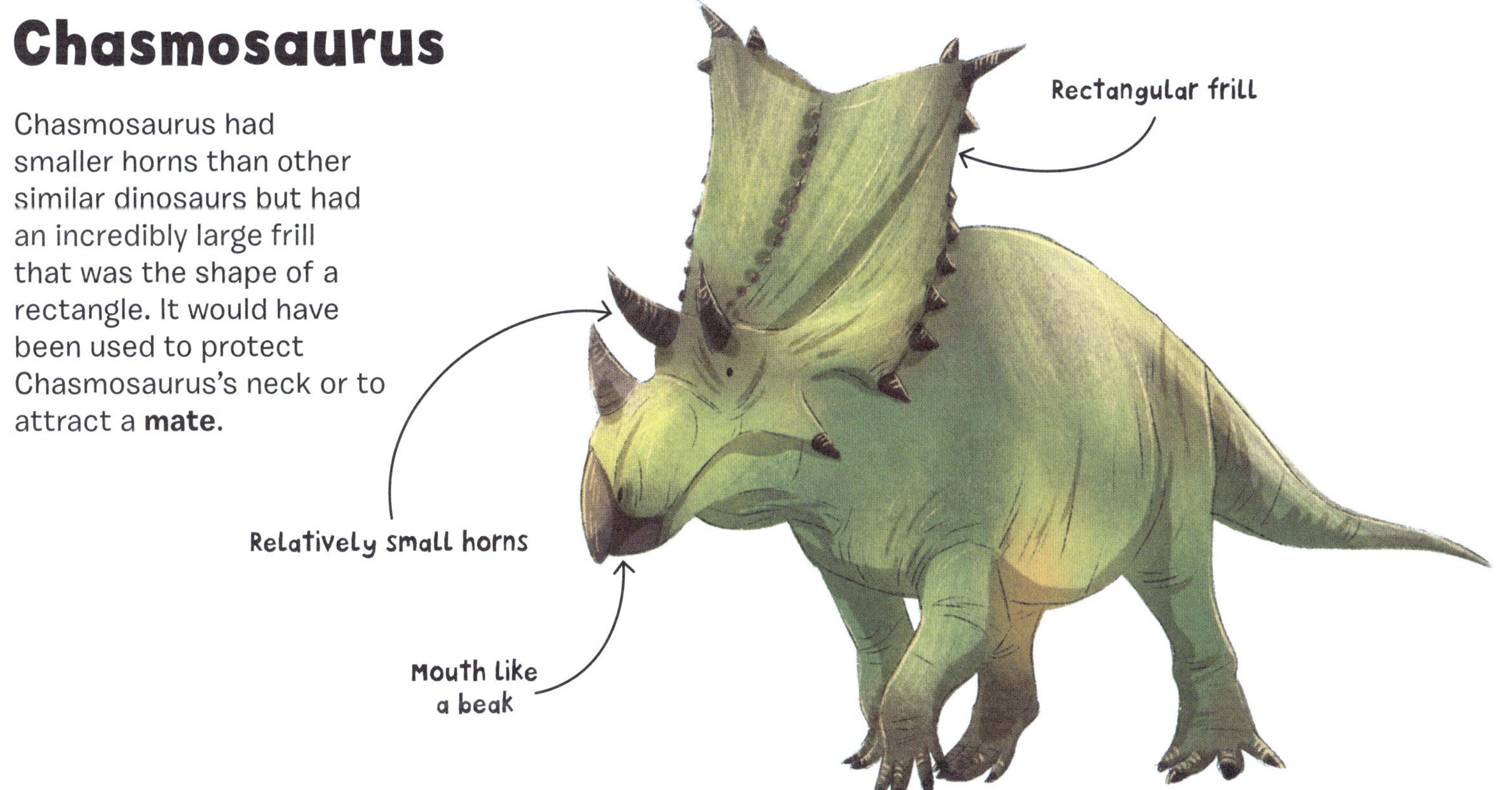

PRONUNCIATION: KAZ-mo-sore-us

DIET: Herbivore

TIME PERIOD: Late Cretaceous

SIZE

SPEED

DEADLY RATING

Stegouros

Stegouros was related to dinosaurs like Ankylosaurus (page 31) but had a slightly different tail. Stegouros's was wide and flat rather than rounded, and would have been waved from side to side to scare predators.

Tough bones sticking out for protection

Short, flat club tail

Stocky body

PRONUNCIATION: ste-GOR-os

DIET: Herbivore

TIME PERIOD: Late Cretaceous

SIZE	
SPEED	
DEADLY RATING	

Kosmoceratops

While Lokiceratops (page 39) had the longest frill horns of any horned dinosaur, Kosmoceratops had the most! This made it one of the most impressive dinosaurs to look at!

PRONUNCIATION: COS-mo-SER-ah-tops

DIET: Herbivore

TIME PERIOD: Late Cretaceous

SIZE	
SPEED	
DEADLY RATING	

Lokiceratops

Lokiceratops looked similar to a modern-day rhinoceros! It had the largest frill horns of any horned dinosaur ever, but would have used these for attracting mates or to intimidate other dinosaurs of the same species rather than for fighting.

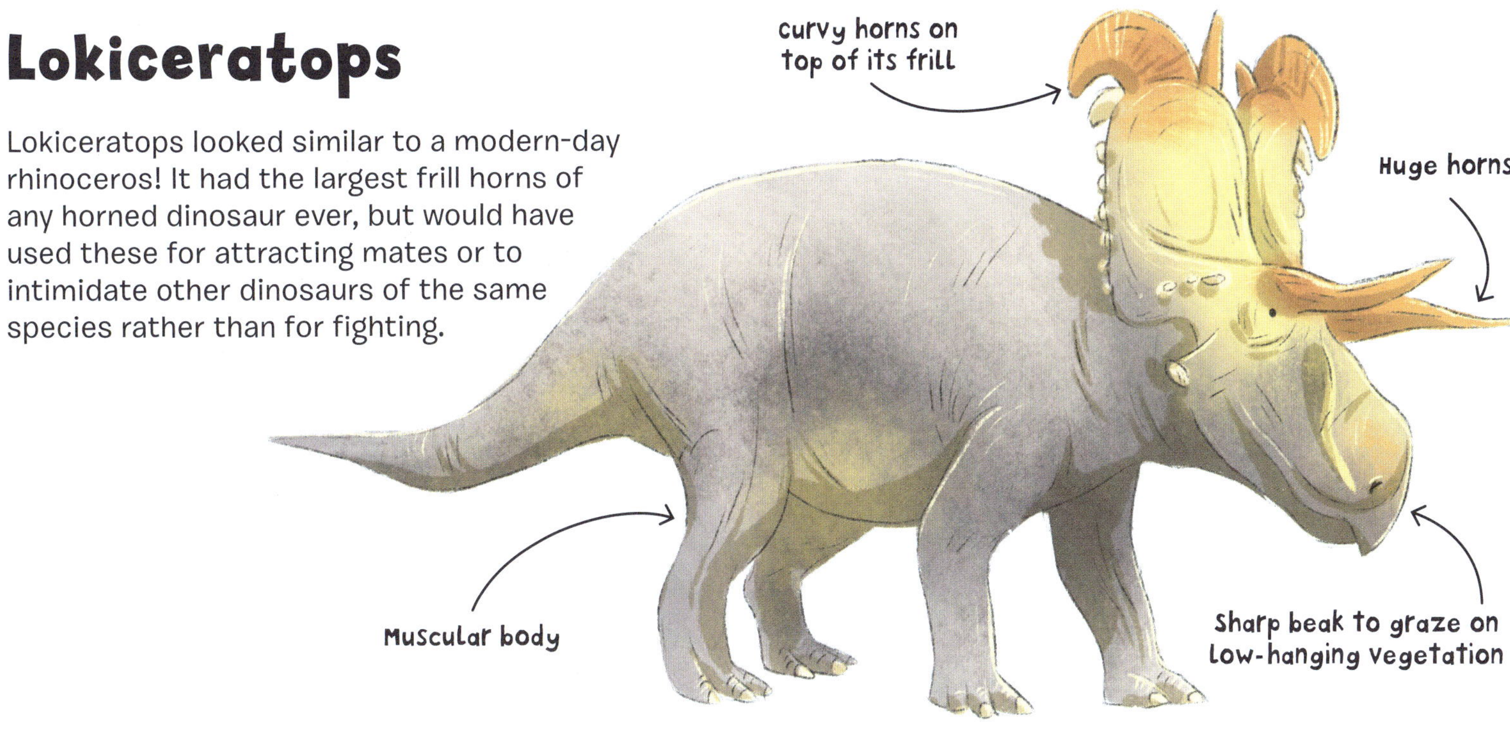

PRONUNCIATION: lo-KEY-ser-ah-tops	SIZE
DIET: Herbivore	SPEED
TIME PERIOD: Late Cretaceous	DEADLY RATING

Huayangosaurus

An early cousin of Stegosaurus (page 69), Huayangosaurus had two rows of rigid, spiky plates sticking up from its back. It also had several spikes near the end of its tail to use if any larger predator got too close.

PRONUNCIATION: hoy-YANG-oh-SORE-us	SIZE
DIET: Herbivore	SPEED
TIME PERIOD: Mid Jurassic	DEADLY RATING

Lambeosaurus

Lambeosaurus was a type of 'duck-billed' dinosaur, a group of dinosaurs that got their names because of their flattened snouts. Despite the shape of its snout, Lambeosaurus still had a lot of teeth, which it could quickly and easily replace if any got worn down while chewing on plants.

PRONUNCIATION: lam-BEE-oh-SORE-us

DIET: Herbivore

TIME PERIOD: Late Cretaceous

SIZE	
SPEED	
DEADLY RATING	

Styracosaurus

The defining feature of Styracosaurus was its impressive nose horn that looked like a rhino's. It was a heavy dinosaur and likely not very fast. Because it couldn't run away from large predators, it instead found safety in numbers and lived in herds to protect itself.

PRONUNCIATION: sty-RAK-oh-sore-us

DIET: Herbivore

TIME PERIOD: Late Cretaceous

SIZE	
SPEED	
DEADLY RATING	

Gastonia

This well-protected dinosaur had two especially large spikes over its shoulders. It lacked the club tail of its relatives but it still had the tough appearance to avoid attacks from other dinosaurs.

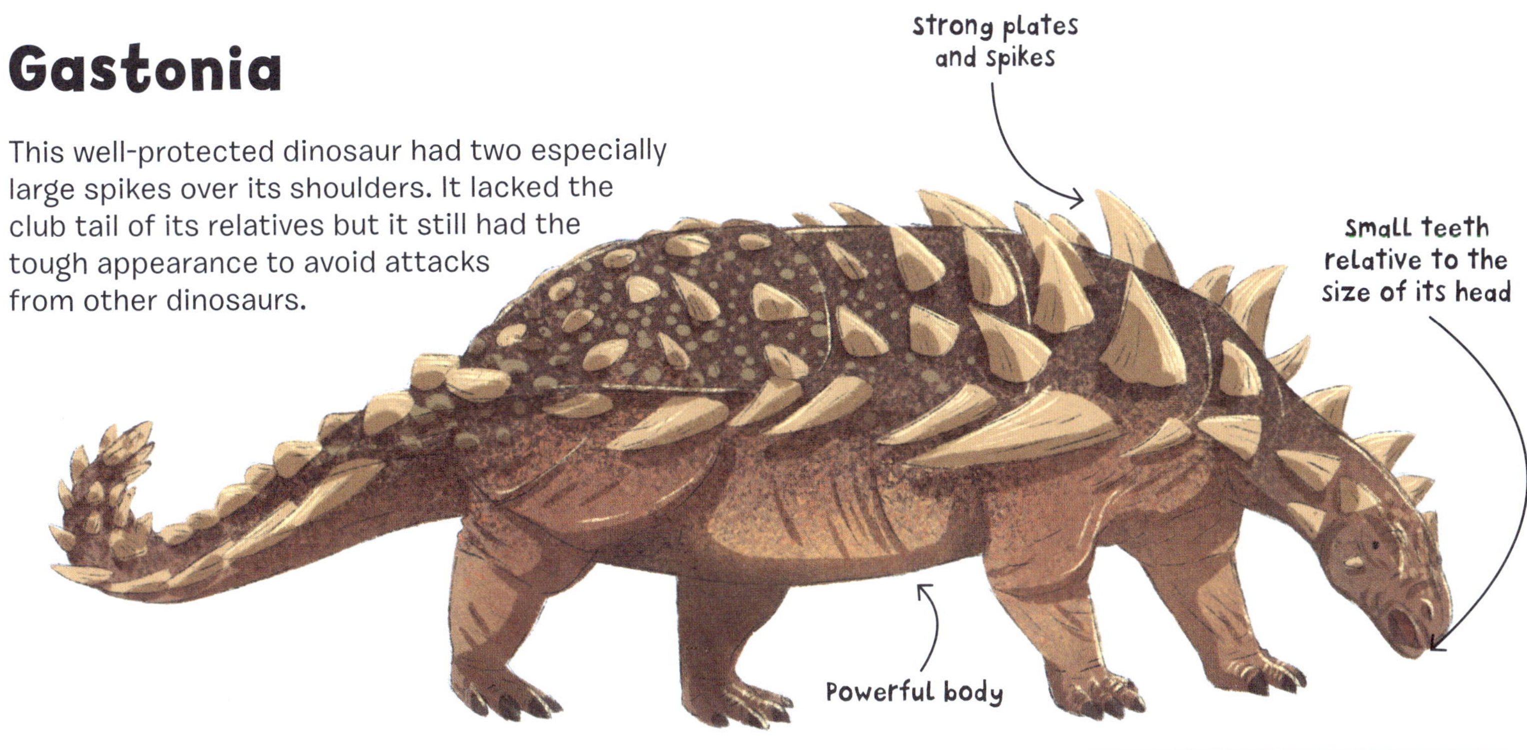

PRONUNCIATION: gas-TOH-nee-ah

DIET: Herbivore

TIME PERIOD: Early Cretaceous

SIZE

SPEED

DEADLY RATING

Ouranosaurus

Ouranosaurus is another duck-billed dinosaur like Lambeosaurus (page 40). It had rows of tightly-packed teeth ideal for chomping on vegetation and could rear up on its back legs to reach any food higher up.

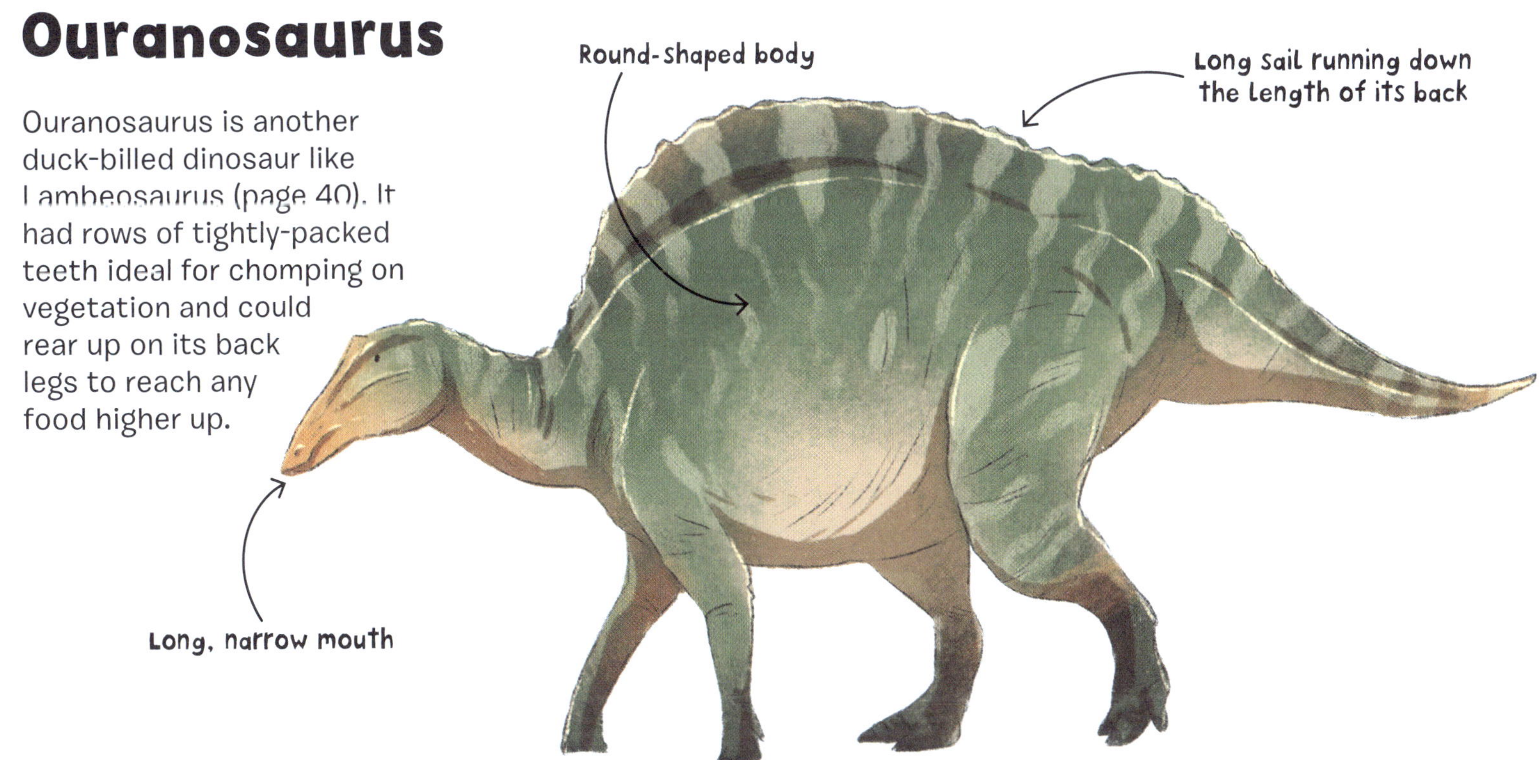

PRONUNCIATION: oo-RAH-noh-sore-us

DIET: Herbivore

TIME PERIOD: Early Cretaceous

SIZE

SPEED

DEADLY RATING

Nodosaurus

Unlike most of its relatives, Nodosaurus didn't have protective spikes on its head or a tail like a club. It did, however, have the usual tough protective plates across its body. Because of its short neck, it would have only eaten from vegetation close to the floor.

PRONUNCIATION: no-doh-SORE-us

DIET: Herbivore

TIME PERIOD: Early Cretaceous

SIZE

SPEED

DEADLY RATING

Einiosaurus

Einiosaurus shared many traits with other Ceratopsian dinosaurs, including a large frill with horns on top, and a muscular body. However, the horn on Einiosaurus's nose curved downward rather than up. This would have made it difficult to use in a fight against a predator.

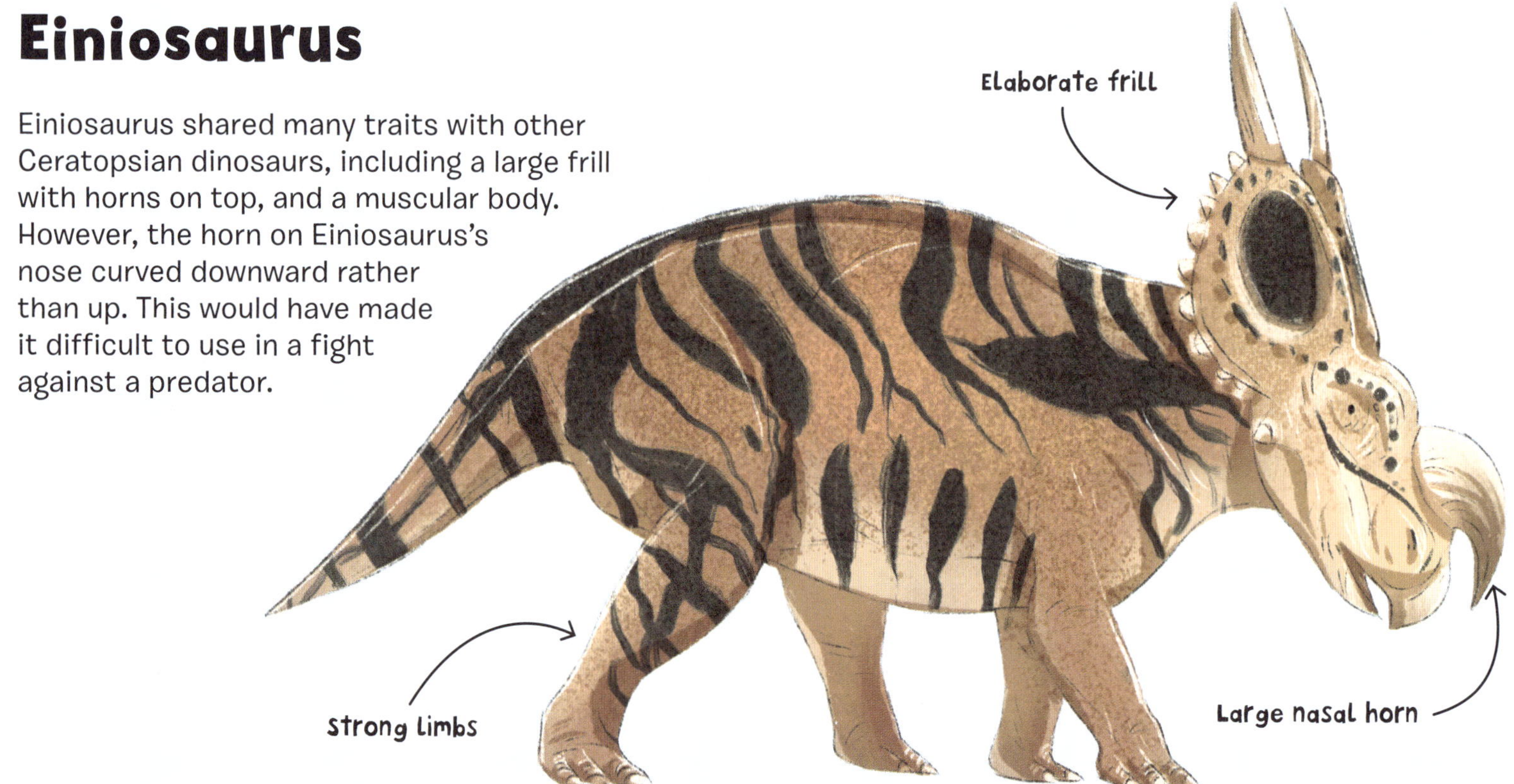

PRONUNCIATION: EE-nee-oh-sore-us

DIET: Herbivore

TIME PERIOD: Late Cretaceous

SIZE

SPEED

DEADLY RATING

Amargasaurus

The double row of spines along its neck and body gave Amargasaurus a distinctive appearance! What they looked like exactly is still a mystery to science. They could have been individual spikes or horns, or connected by skin like a **sail**.

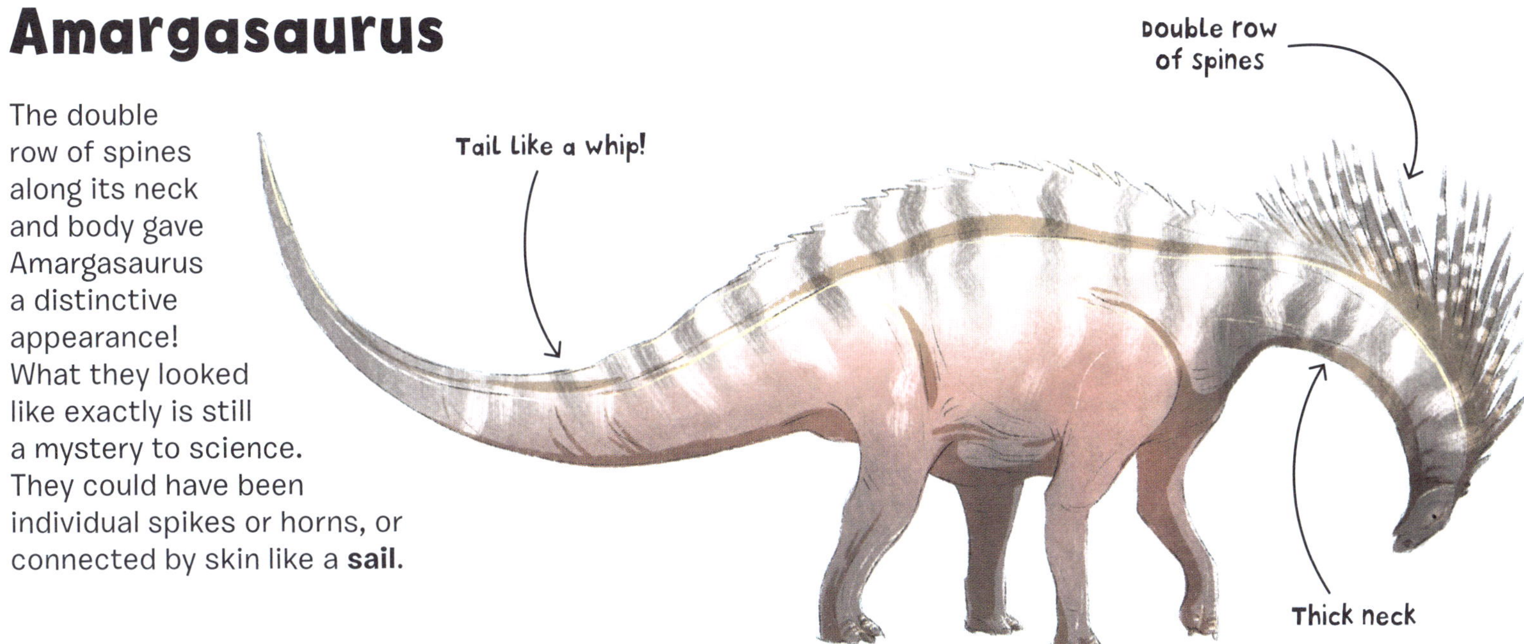

PRONUNCIATION: A-MARG-oh-sore-us

DIET: Herbivore

TIME PERIOD: Early Cretaceous

SIZE

SPEED

DEADLY RATING

Eotrachodon

Eotrachodon went about its life on a mixture of two and four legs. Scientists think it walked around mainly on its strong back legs, but came down onto all fours to eat.

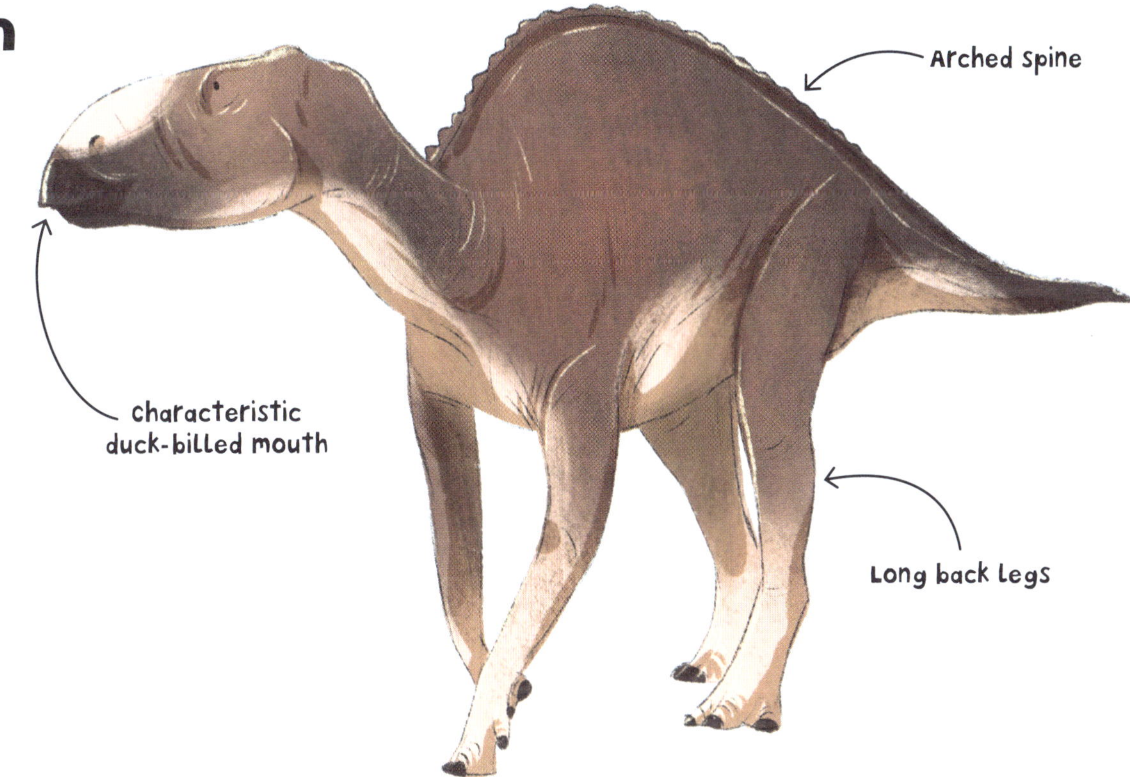

PRONUNCIATION: ee-OH-trak-oh-don

DIET: Herbivore

TIME PERIOD: Late Cretaceous

SIZE

SPEED

DEADLY RATING

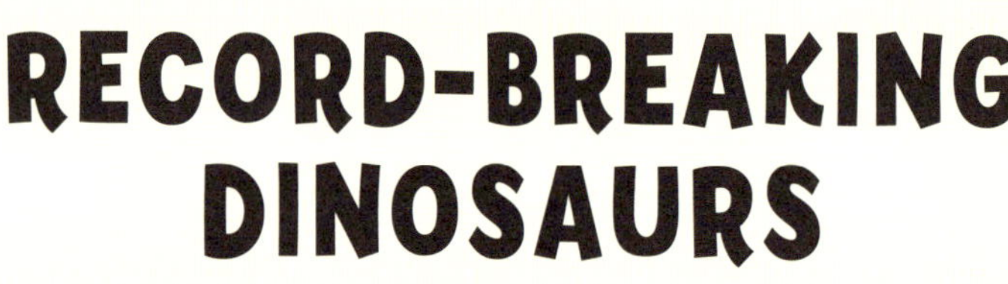

RECORD-BREAKING DINOSAURS

Some dinosaurs were born to break records. These incredible creatures pushed the limits of nature using their strength, size, and speed. Whether they soared through the skies at breakneck speeds or prowled across the land on massive legs, the dinosaurs in this chapter have all gone down in history!

Megalosaurus

When Megalosaurus was first discovered, scientists thought it was a large lizard because no one knew what dinosaurs were yet! That's why its name simply means "great lizard". It was the first dinosaur to ever be named.

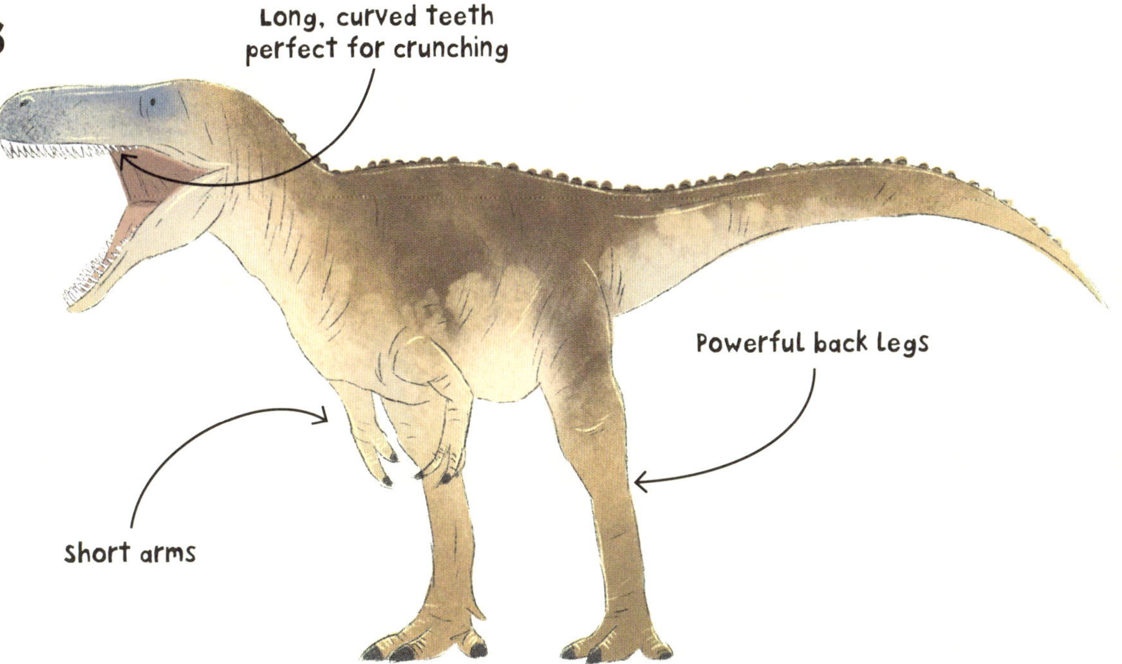

PRONUNCIATION: MEG-ah-low-sore-us

DIET: Carnivore

TIME PERIOD: Mid Jurassic

SIZE

SPEED

DEADLY RATING

Tail held horizontally behind it

Procompsognathus

This speedy dinosaur was the smallest dinosaur ever found at the time – although even smaller ones have been found since. It preyed on insects and small mammals using clawed hands that were relatively big compared to the rest of its body.

PRONUNCIATION: pro-comp-sog-NAY-thus

DIET: Carnivore

TIME PERIOD: Late Triassic

SIZE	
SPEED	
DEADLY RATING	

Brachiosaurus

The huge Brachiosaurus had very upright posture, preferring to hold its neck high in the air rather than out in front of it. It had a tiny head and an even tinier brain, and would have needed to spend most of the day eating just to get enough energy to survive.

PRONUNCIATION: BRAK-ee-oh-sore-us

DIET: Herbivore

TIME PERIOD: Late Jurassic

SIZE	  
SPEED	
DEADLY RATING	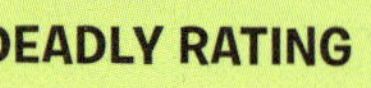  

Diplodocus

This dinosaur was one of the longest of all, thanks to its incredible neck and tail. Its neck allowed it to eat vegetation high above the ground in the **prehistoric** treetops, while its tail could be whipped from side to side to fend off predators.

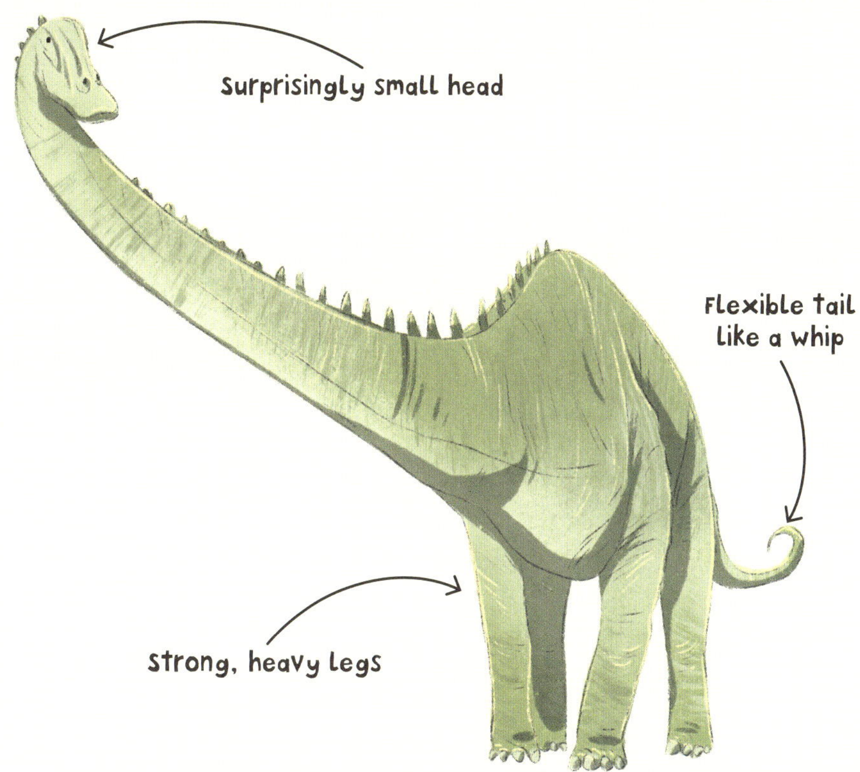

PRONUNCIATION: dih-PLOD-uh-kus

DIET: Herbivore

TIME PERIOD: Late Jurassic

SIZE

SPEED

DEADLY RATING

Quetzalcoatlus

Quetzalcoatlus is the largest flying animal of all time! It was the size of a giraffe, but that didn't stop it from leaping into the air and beating its massive wings to take off into the skies. It flew above rivers and oceans in search of fish and other small marine creatures to eat.

PRONUNCIATION: ket-suhl-kow-AT-luhs

DIET: Carnivore

TIME PERIOD: Late Cretaceous

SIZE

SPEED

DEADLY RATING

Because of the shape of its head and mouth, scientists initially thought Oculudentavis was a bird!

Oculudentavis

Even though its name means "eye-tooth-bird", scientists now believe that this creature was more like a lizard. It was extremely small and was the same size as a modern-day hummingbird. It had very big eyes and lots of teeth!

PRONUNCIATION: oh-cue-lu-den-TAH-viss

DIET: Carnivore

TIME PERIOD: Late Cretaceous

SIZE

SPEED

DEADLY RATING

Argentinosaurus

Argentinosaurus is one of the largest land animals to ever walk the Earth! It used its long neck to feast on plants that most other dinosaurs could not reach. But because of its sheer size, it was very slow. It had to rely on its bulk being enough to scare off any predators.

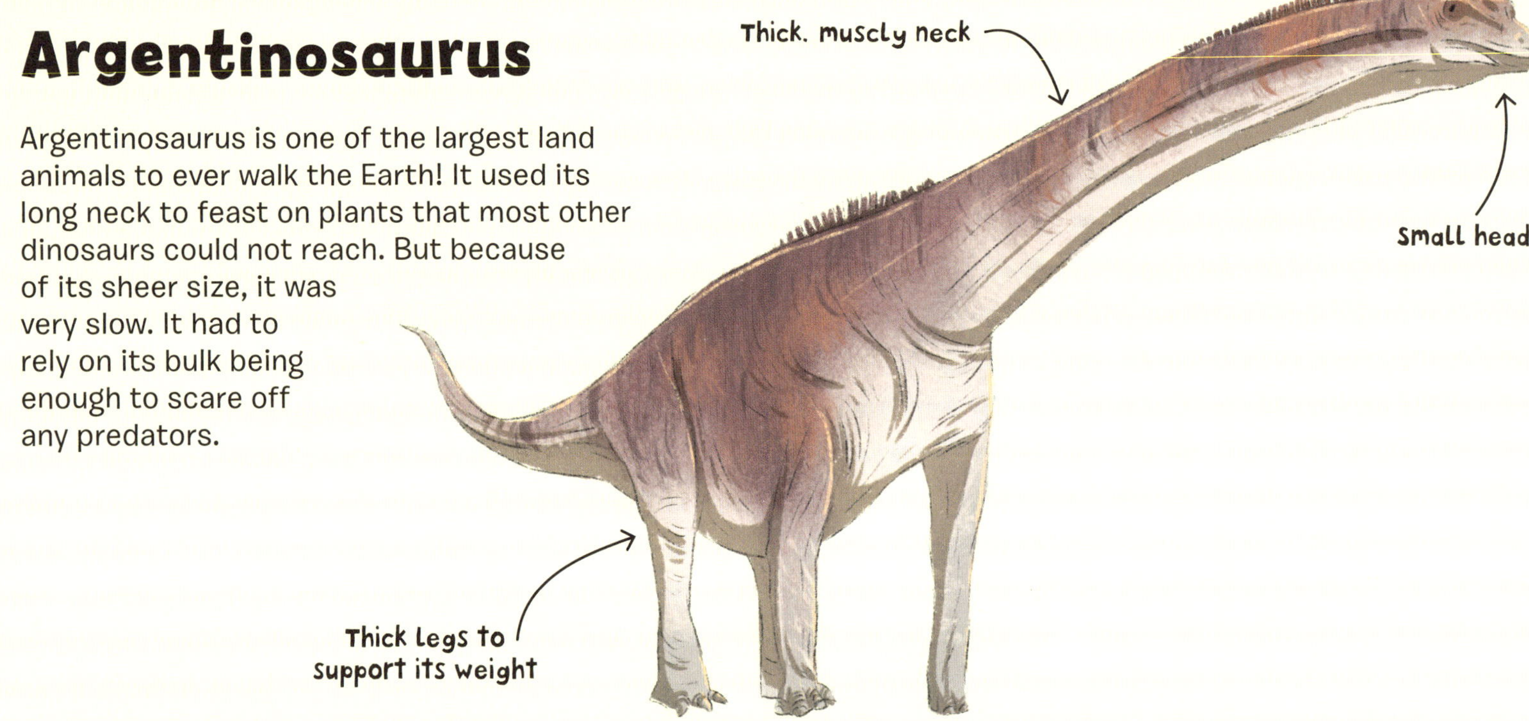

PRONUNCIATION: AR-gen-TEE-no-SORE-us

DIET: Herbivore

TIME PERIOD: Late Cretaceous

SIZE

SPEED

DEADLY RATING

Gallimimus

The speedy Gallimimus was over twice as fast as the average human. Having its eyes positioned more on the side of its head gave it a wide field of vision and meant it could spot any predators trying to sneak up on it, and sprint away before they could strike.

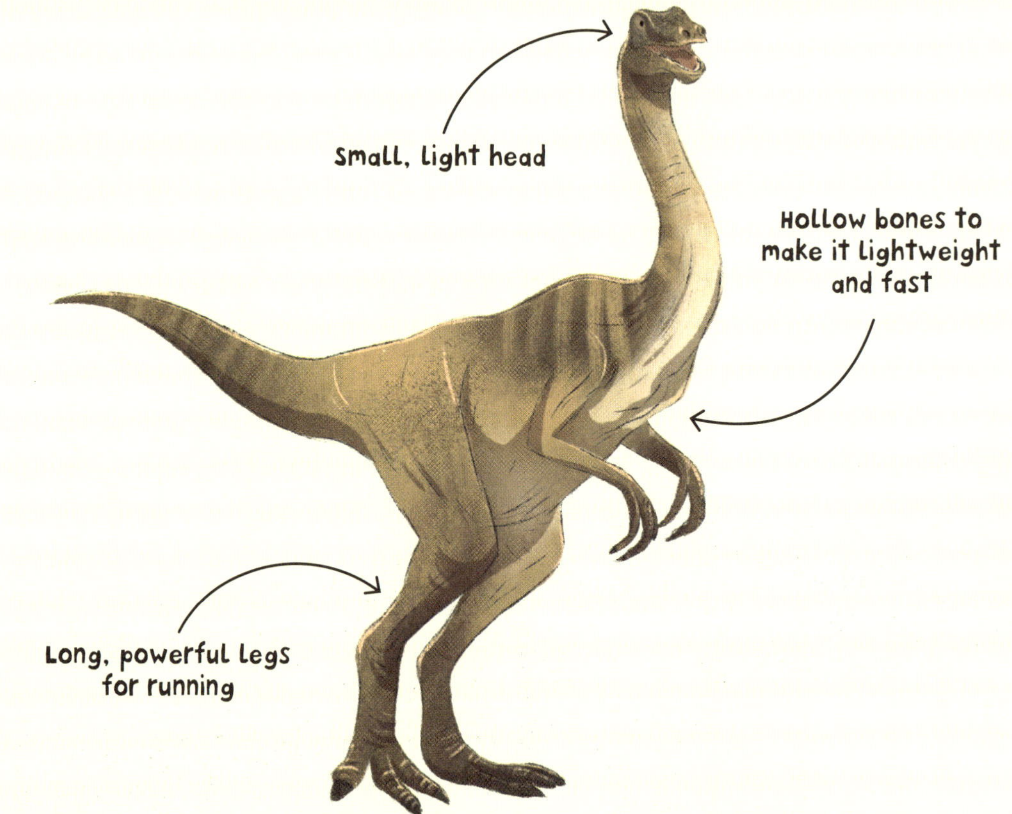

PRONUNCIATION: galley-MIME-us

DIET: Omnivore

TIME PERIOD: Late Cretaceous

SIZE

SPEED

DEADLY RATING

Vectaerovenator

Vectaerovenator possessed sharp claws and strong back legs. Large air spaces were found in its bones, which suggested it would have had a very light skeleton that made it nimble and agile.

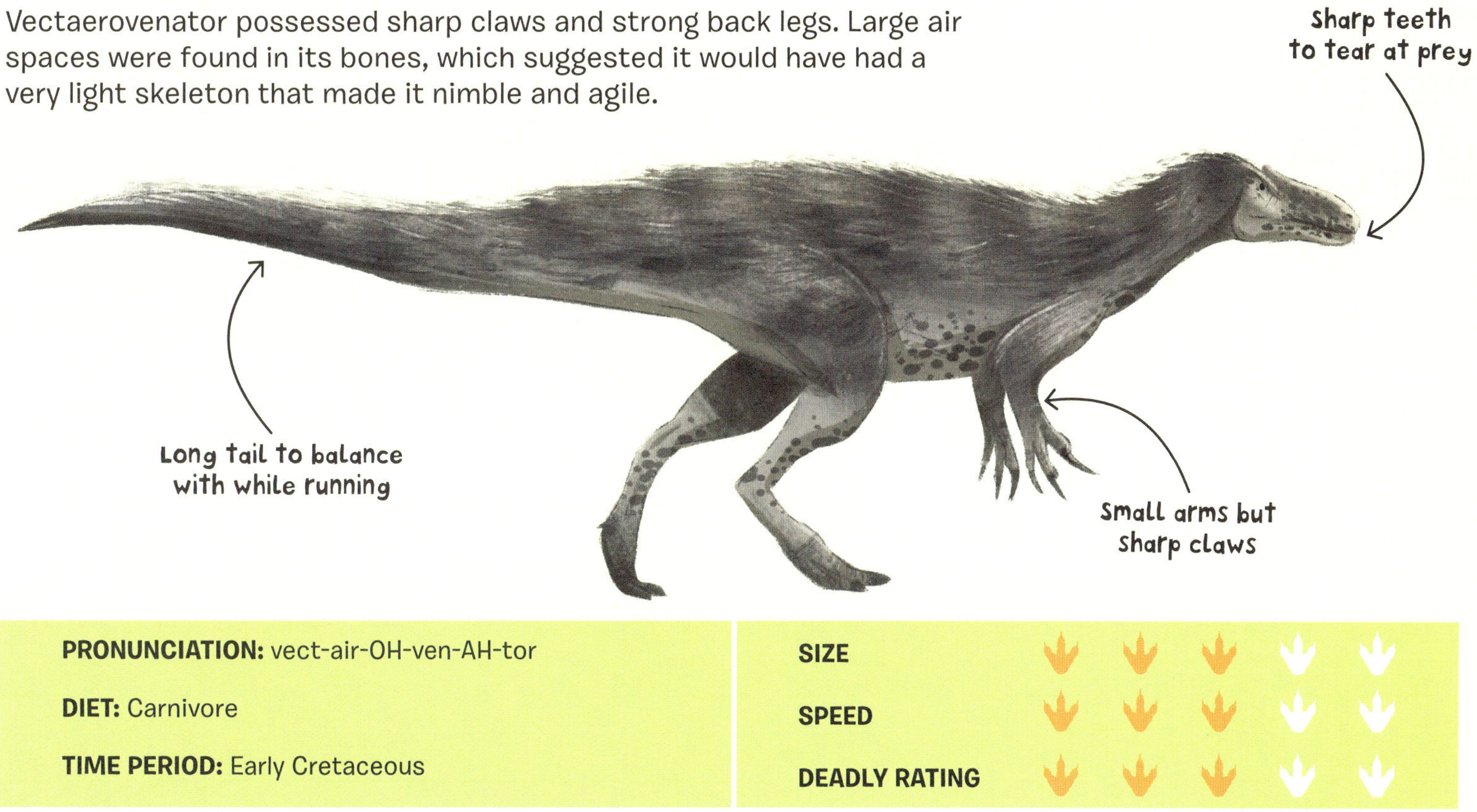

PRONUNCIATION: vect-air-OH-ven-AH-tor

DIET: Carnivore

TIME PERIOD: Early Cretaceous

SIZE

SPEED

DEADLY RATING

Oryctodromeus

The unusual Oryctodromeus is the only known burrowing dinosaur! It dug its way underground using its sharp claws to create dens to shelter in during the winter, and to hide from predators.

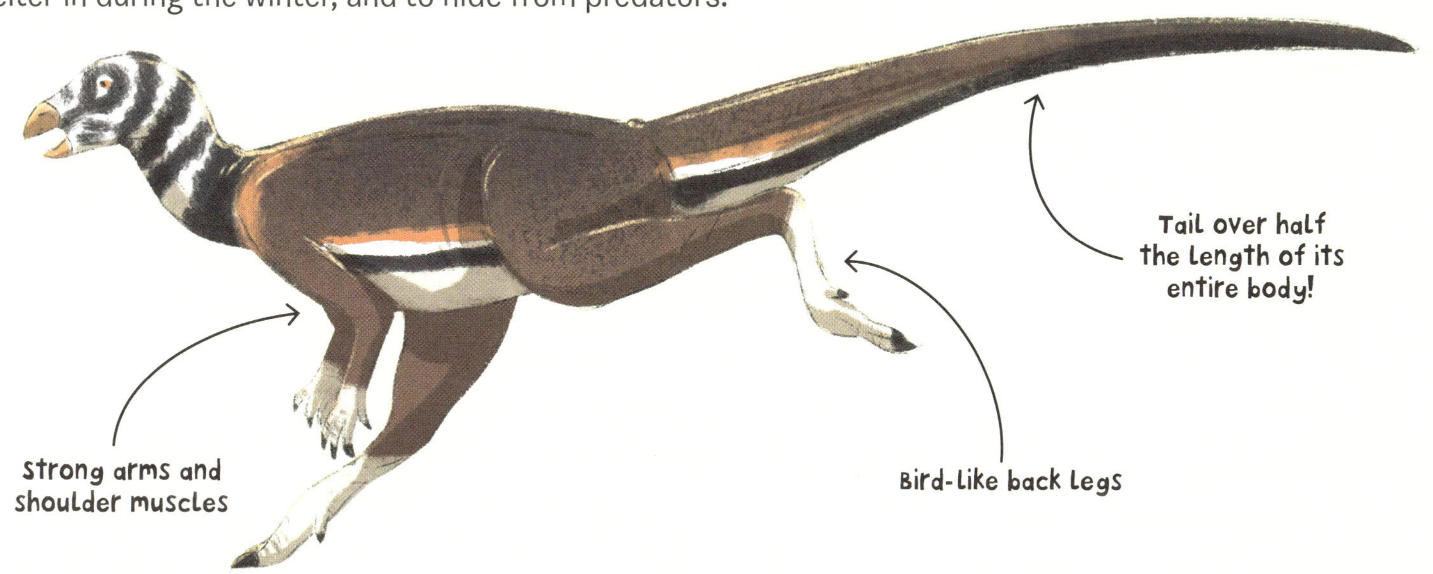

PRONUNCIATION: or-IK-tow-DROHM-ee-us

DIET: Herbivore

TIME PERIOD: Late Cretaceous

SIZE

SPEED

DEADLY RATING

Eoraptor

Eoraptor is one of the oldest known dinosaurs. It was relatively small – about the same size as a medium-sized dog – and walked on its back legs. It took advantage of having hollow bones to chase quickly after its prey.

PRONUNCIATION: EE-oh-RAP-tor

DIET: Carnivore

TIME PERIOD: Late Triassic

SIZE	2/5
SPEED	4/5
DEADLY RATING	3/5

Sharp teeth for gripping prey

Long legs

Herrerasaurus

Herrerasaurus was likely one of the first dinosaurs to roam the Earth. It pinned down its prey with its talons, opening its jaws very wide to use its backward-curving teeth to tear at skin and bone.

PRONUNCIATION: herr-ray-rah-SORE-us		**SIZE**	
DIET: Carnivore		**SPEED**	
TIME PERIOD: Late Triassic		**DEADLY RATING**	

Mamenchisaurus

Mamenchisaurus had the longest neck relative to its body size of any dinosaur. It was five times longer than a giraffe's neck, and as long as a bus! Mamenchisaurus needed to have a very large heart to be able to pump blood all the way up to its head.

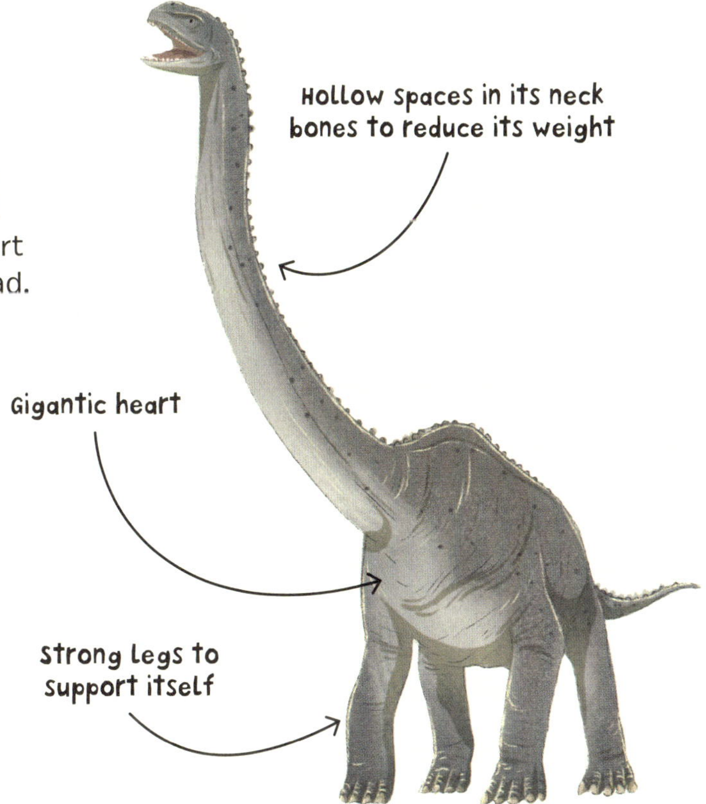

PRONUNCIATION: mah-men-chi-SORE-us		**SIZE**	
DIET: Herbivore		**SPEED**	
TIME PERIOD: Late Jurassic		**DEADLY RATING**	  

Archaeopteryx

Archaeopteryx is described as the "missing link" between birds and dinosaurs. It had a small frame and feathered wings like a bird. But it also had sharp teeth and a bony tail like a dinosaur. It can teach scientists a lot about about how dinosaurs and the birds that live on Earth in the present day are related!

PRONUNCIATION: AR-kee-op-TE-rix	SIZE
DIET: Carnivore	SPEED
TIME PERIOD: Late Jurassic	DEADLY RATING

Sauroposeidon

The neck bones of this dinosaur were so large, they were mistaken for the trunks of prehistoric trees when they were first discovered! Each bone was the same size as a fridge, and its neck overall was only slightly shorter than Mamenchisaurus's (page 53).

PRONUNCIATION: saw-ro-poh-SIE-don	SIZE   
DIET: Herbivore	SPEED
TIME PERIOD: Early Cretaceous	DEADLY RATING 

Torosaurus

Scientists initially thought Torosaurus was just an adult Triceratops (page 32). They did look very similar! But Torosaurus is actually its own species, and had the largest skull of any land-based animal ever! It likely lived and roamed in groups for protection against predators.

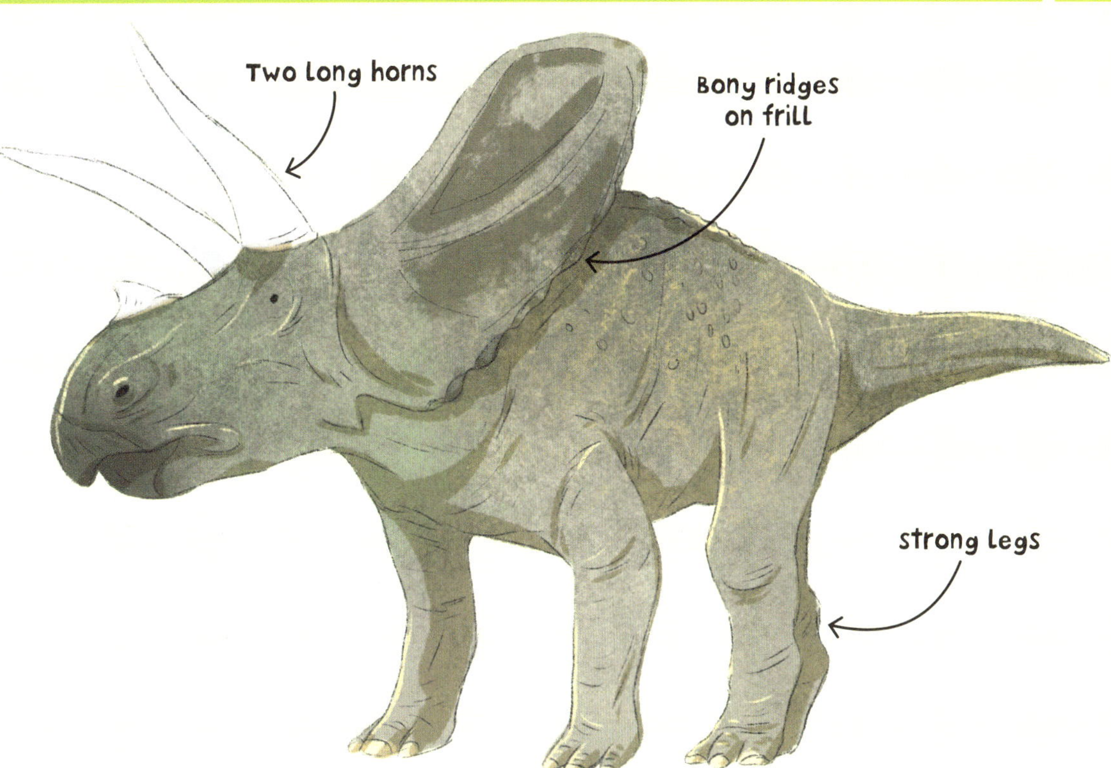

PRONUNCIATION: tor-oh-SORE-us	SIZE
DIET: Herbivore	SPEED
TIME PERIOD: Late Cretaceous	DEADLY RATING

Confuciusornis

Confuciusornis was a very small bird-like dinosaur, no bigger than a hardback book! It had strong, light, intricate feathers, including two very long ones that trailed out behind its tail. It is the earliest known creature of its kind.

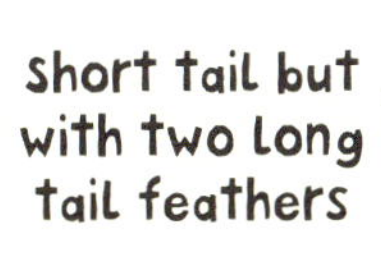

PRONUNCIATION: kon-FEW-shus-or-niss	SIZE	  
DIET: Carnivore	SPEED	
TIME PERIOD: Early Cretaceous	DEADLY RATING	

Pteranodon

One of the largest flying reptiles ever discovered, Pteranodon had a huge wingspan that made it great at gliding. It soared through the skies above the oceans, with giant jaws like a pelican's that it could open wide and scoop up fish or other small marine creatures.

Relatively large eyes for spotting prey

Powerful shoulders used to flap its huge wings

Long, scoop-like jaws with no teeth

PRONUNCIATION: teh-ran-OH-don	**SIZE**
DIET: Carnivore	**SPEED**
TIME PERIOD: Late Cretaceous	**DEADLY RATING**

Alamosaurus

Despite having a small brain, Alamosaurus was still smart enough to know how to use its long neck to its advantage. It didn't waste energy moving its entire body from place to place in search of new food. Instead, it stayed in one spot and used its neck to reach places it hadn't yet eaten from.

PRONUNCIATION: ah-la-mow-SORE-us	**SIZE**  
DIET: Herbivore	**SPEED** 
TIME PERIOD: Late Cretaceous	**DEADLY RATING** 

Chenanisaurus

Chenanisaurus is a very rare dinosaur, and is believed to be one of the last to roam the Earth! It existed at the same time as Tyrannosaurus rex (page 13) and had a similar powerful bite with very small arms. However, the two lived on different continents and wouldn't have crossed paths.

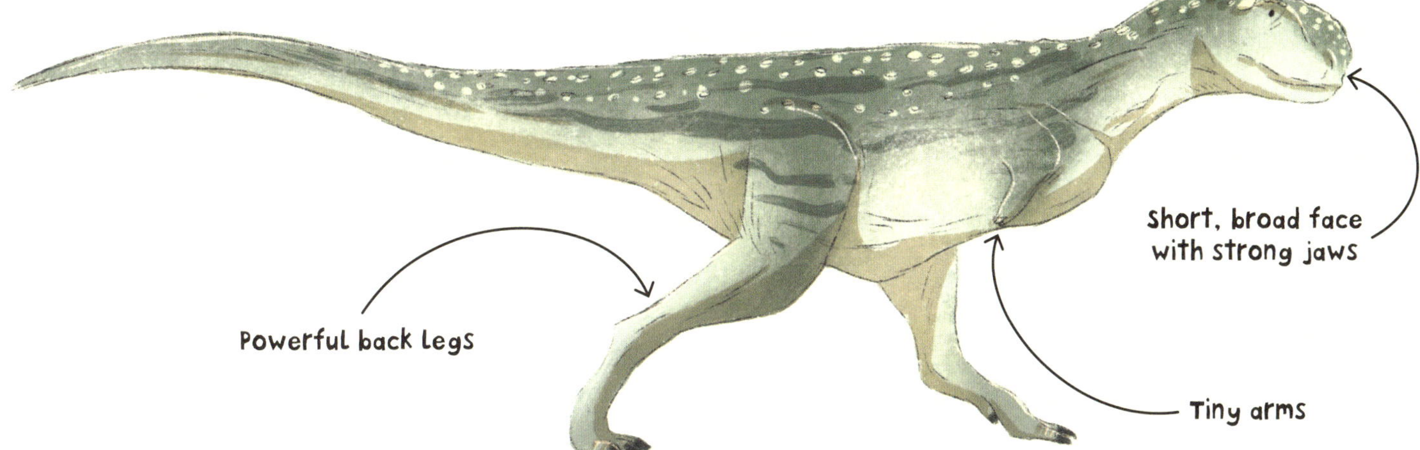

PRONUNCIATION: chen-an-ee-SORE-us

DIET: Carnivore

TIME PERIOD: Late Cretaceous

SIZE	3 of 5
SPEED	3 of 5
DEADLY RATING	3 of 5

Musankwa

Musankwa came from a group of plant-eating dinosaurs that all have small heads and long necks. While they were small to medium in size, scientists think that they later grew into the largest of all the land-based dinosaurs. Musankwa could teach us a lot about those giants!

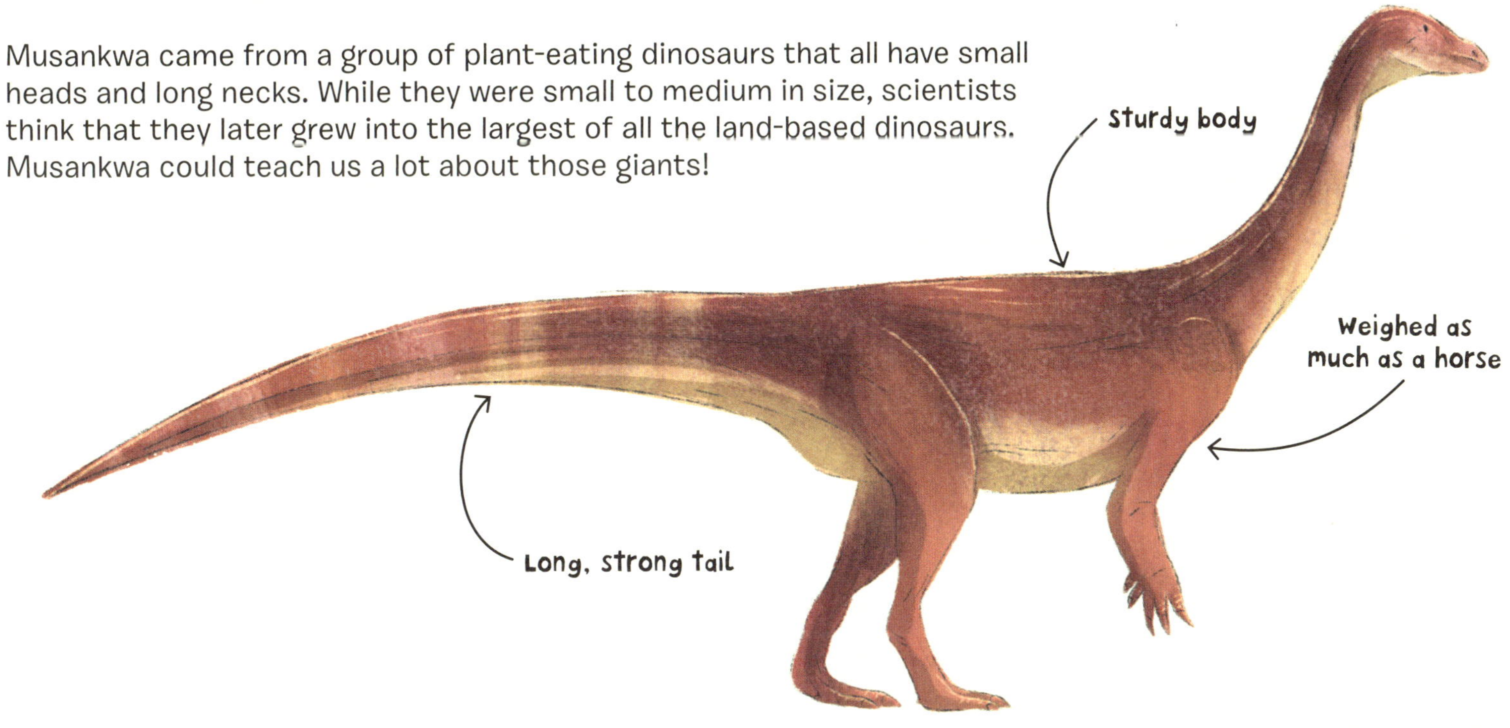

PRONUNCIATION: MOO-san-kwah

DIET: Herbivore

TIME PERIOD: Late Triassic

SIZE	3 of 5
SPEED	3 of 5
DEADLY RATING	3 of 5

Yi Qi

Yi Qi was part of a group of dinosaurs that are closely related to modern-day birds. It had featherless wings and was capable of flying short distances between tree branches or gliding from those branches down to the ground. It was very, very small – only the size of a sparrow!

Small piece of bone sticking out of each wrist

Wings like a bat

Only one Yi Qi fossil has ever been found!

PRONUNCIATION: ee-key	**SIZE**
DIET: Insectivore	**SPEED**
TIME PERIOD: Mid Jurassic	**DEADLY RATING**

Eocarcharia

Eocarcharia had what looked like a bony eyebrow above each eye and had incredible blade-like teeth. These teeth would have made it a deadly opponent in a battle – no wonder it was one of the top predators of its day!

PRONUNCIATION: ee-oh-car-CAR-ee-ah	**SIZE**   
DIET: Carnivore	**SPEED**  
TIME PERIOD: Early Cretaceous	**DEADLY RATING** 

Patagotitan

Patagotitan may have been the same length as the incredibly long Diplodocus (page 47), but it was also twice as tall and over three times as heavy! It was one of the largest dinosaurs ever to walk the Earth.

PRONUNCIATION: pat-ah-go-TIE-tan

DIET: Herbivore

TIME PERIOD: Early Cretaceous

SIZE 

SPEED 

DEADLY RATING

Pendraig

With a name that means "chief dragon", it may be easy to picture Pendraig as a big, heavy dinosaur. But no, it was actually the size of a chicken! It was still a good hunter though, and preyed on small reptiles using its sharp teeth and talons.

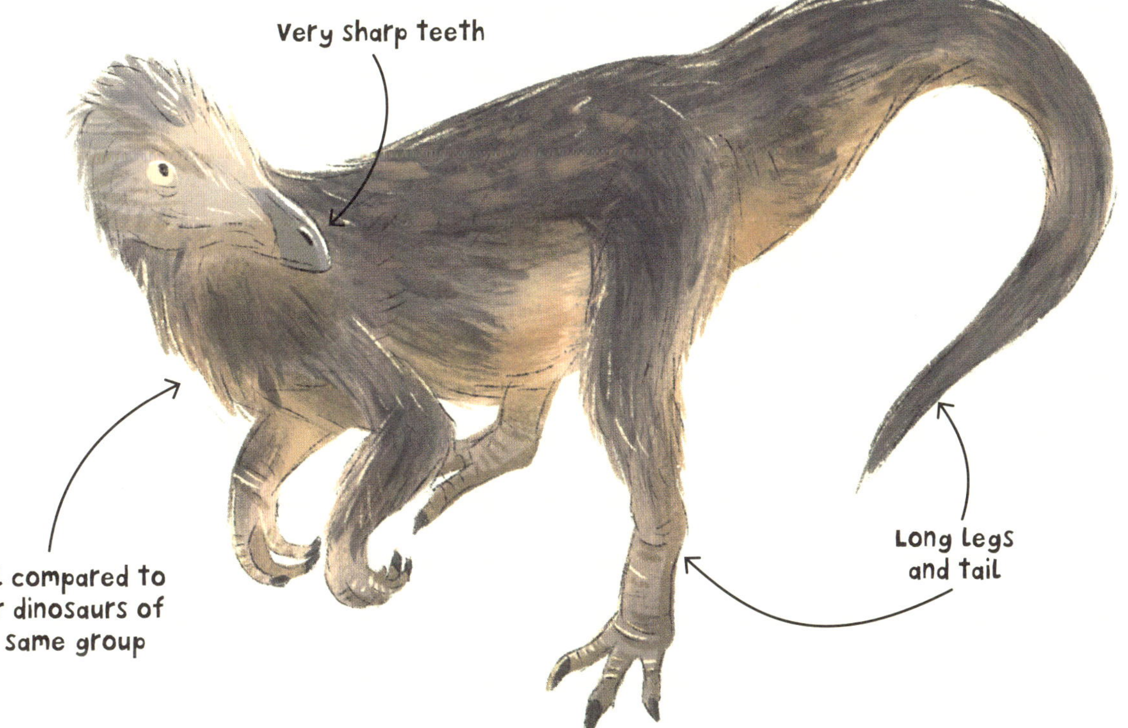

PRONUNCIATION: PEN-dray-g

DIET: Carnivore

TIME PERIOD: Late Triassic

SIZE   

SPEED   

DEADLY RATING  

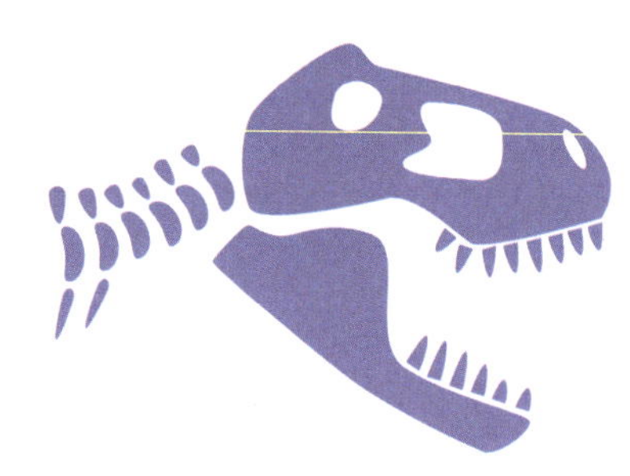

FUNKY-FEATURED DINOSAURS

Dinosaurs came in all shapes and sizes, but some had funky features that set them apart from the rest. Some made loud trumpeting noises to communicate with one another. Others were covered in spikes like a hedgehog! The dinosaurs in this chapter used their unusual features to help them survive in their prehistoric world.

No front teeth!

Muttaburrasaurus

One of this dinosaur's defining features was its large, rounded snout. It may have developed this for two reasons. The first is that it may have made Muttaburrasaurus's sense of smell stronger. The second is that it could have allowed it to make loud calling sounds to communicate with other dinosaurs.

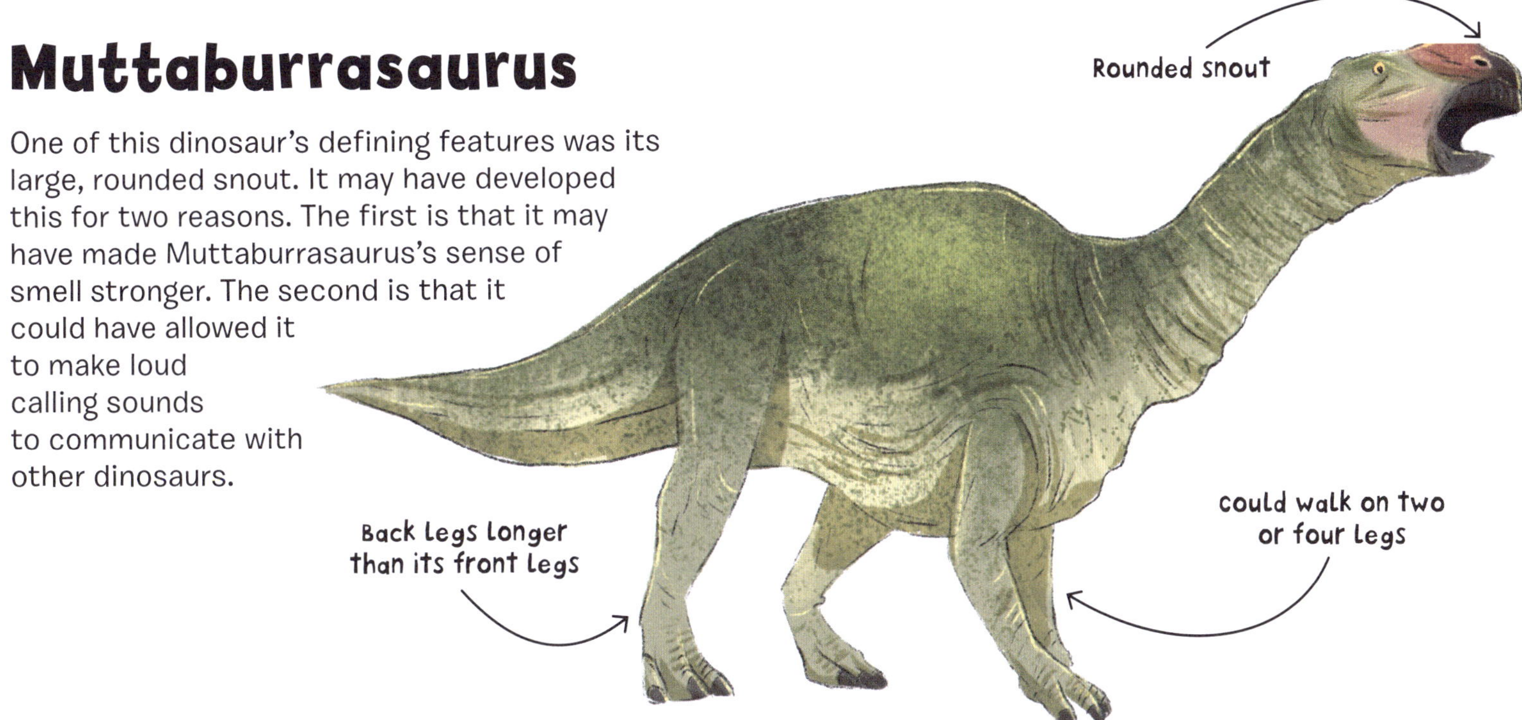

PRONUNCIATION: MUT-a-BURR-a-SORE-us

DIET: Herbivore

TIME PERIOD: Early Cretaceous

SIZE

SPEED

DEADLY RATING

Nigersaurus

Nigersaurus had an incredible 500 teeth, a mixture of visible teeth and ones hidden away to be used as replacements. That's more teeth than any other dinosaur! It used them to munch on lots and lots of vegetation, and has been referred to as the "lawnmower" of the dinosaur world!

PRONUNCIATION: ni-jer-SORE-us

DIET: Herbivore

TIME PERIOD: Early Cretaceous

SIZE

SPEED

DEADLY RATING

Yanornis

Yanornis may look a lot like a modern bird, but unlike the birds we know today it had lots of sharp teeth! While it mainly preferred to eat fish, it did occasionally switch its diet based on the food available around it.

PRONUNCIATION: yah-NOR-niss

DIET: Omnivore

TIME PERIOD: Early Cretaceous

SIZE

SPEED

DEADLY RATING

Gigantoraptor

The largest feathered dinosaur ever found, Gigantoraptor was over twice as tall as a human and almost the same length as a bus! This surprised scientists, as most feathered dinosaurs were very small. It also laid some of the largest dinosaur eggs ever found.

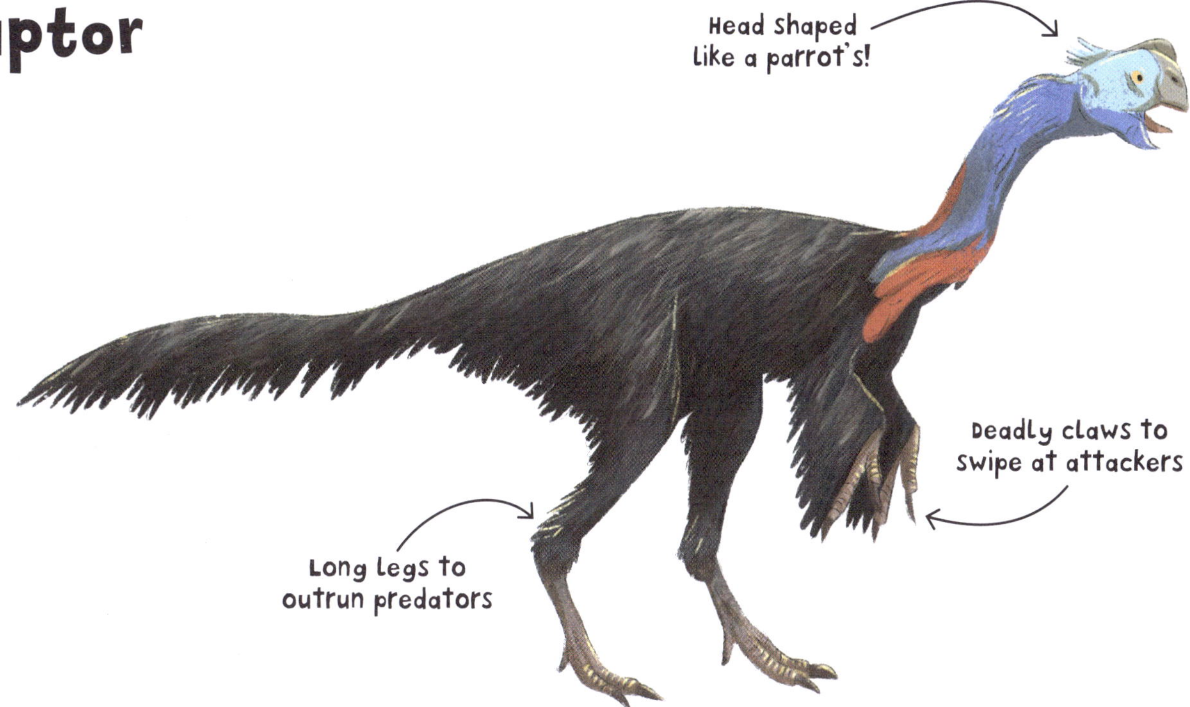

PRONUNCIATION: ji-GAN-to-rap-tor

DIET: Omnivore

TIME PERIOD: Late Cretaceous

SIZE

SPEED

DEADLY RATING

Aquilarhinus

Duck-billed dinosaurs like Aquilarhinus were the most common plant-eating dinosaurs of their time. Their distinctive snouts and jaws were perfectly shaped to scoop up vegetation on the ground. Aquilarhinus also had a crest on its head, although it looked more like a humped nose!

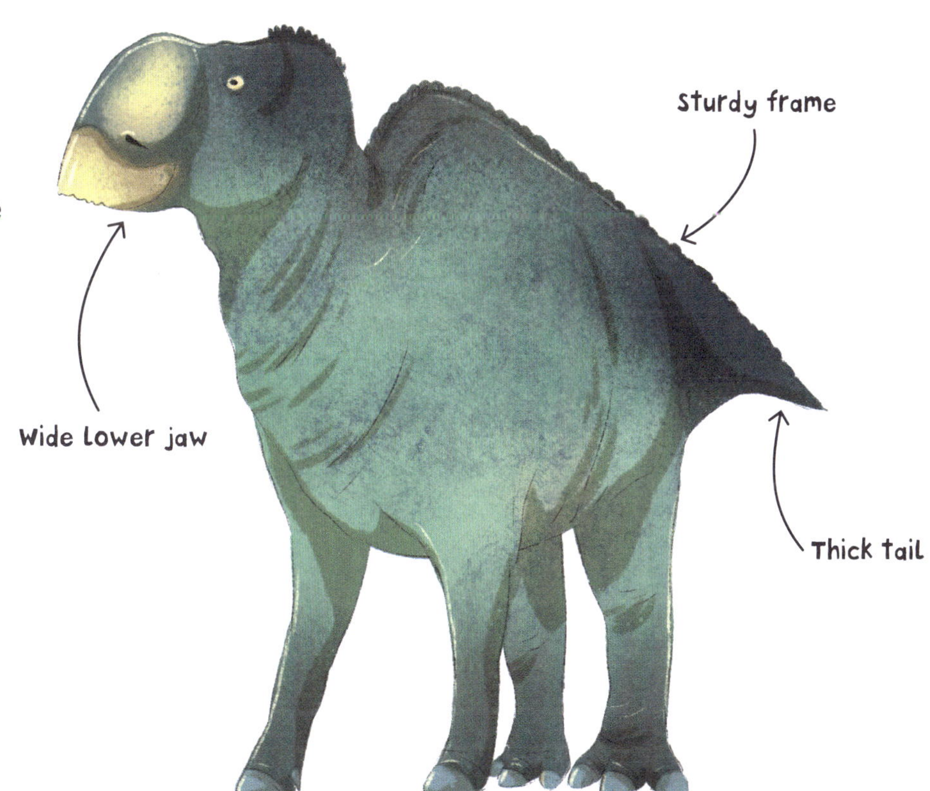

PRONUNCIATION: a-kwi-lar-EE-nuss

DIET: Herbivore

TIME PERIOD: Late Cretaceous

SIZE

SPEED

DEADLY RATING

Epidendrosaurus

The tiny Epidendrosaurus was a tree climber. It used its claws not only to grip onto tree trunks, but also to dig into tiny cracks to reach small insects. Scientists think that it would have been able to glide short distances from one branch to another.

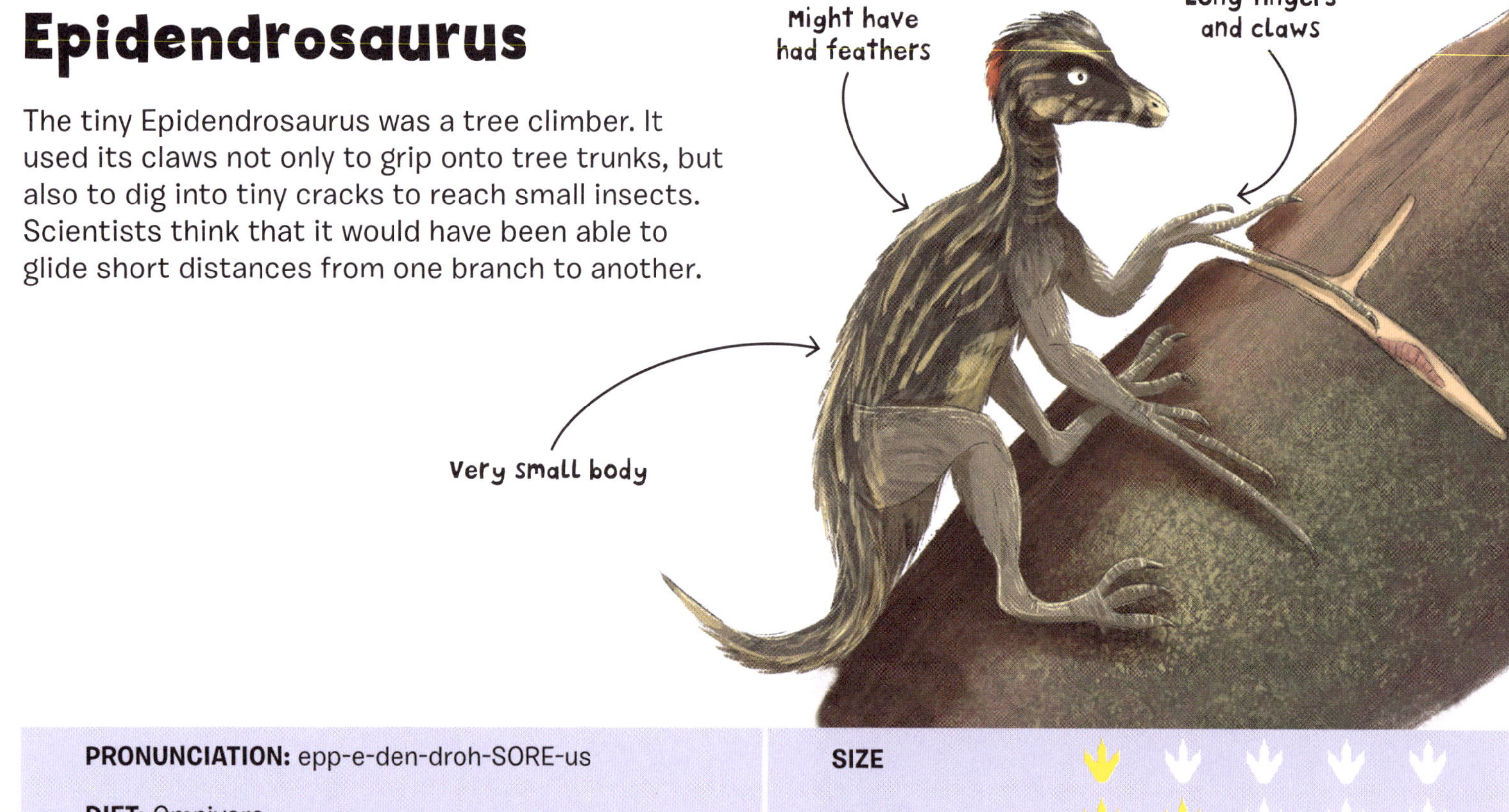

PRONUNCIATION: epp-e-den-droh-SORE-us

DIET: Omnivore

TIME PERIOD: Mid Jurassic

SIZE	●	○	○	○	○
SPEED	●	●	○	○	○
DEADLY RATING	●	○	○	○	○

Iguanodon

The second dinosaur to ever be discovered, Iguanodon had a large spike like a thumb on the end of its front legs. These could have been used to fight back against predators or to strip leaves from branches and make them easier to eat.

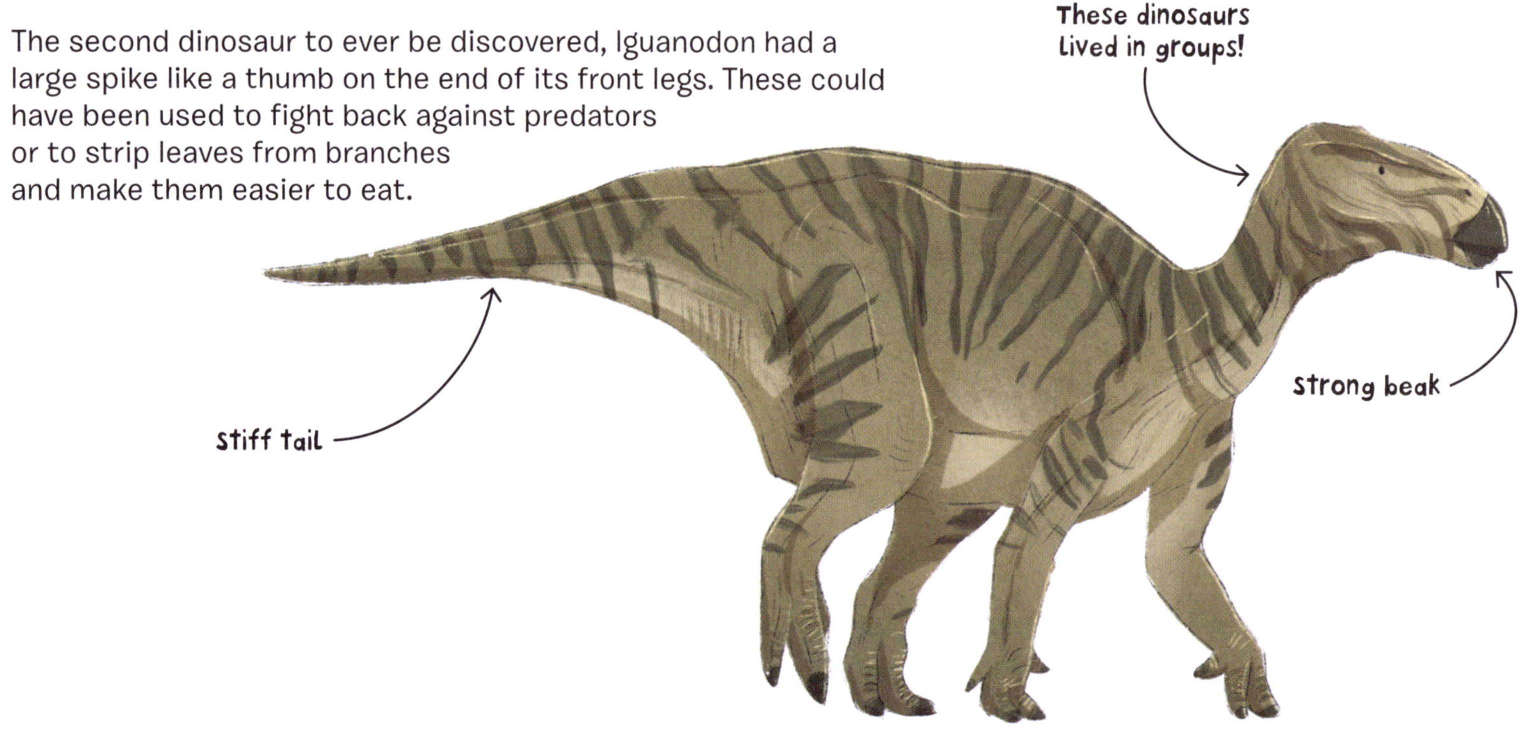

PRONUNCIATION: ig-WHA-noh-don

DIET: Herbivore

TIME PERIOD: Early Cretaceous

SIZE	●	●	●	●	○
SPEED	●	●	●	○	○
DEADLY RATING	●	●	●	○	○

Anatotitan

Considering that its name means “duck titan”, it’s no surprise that Anatotitan was a duck-billed dinosaur. However, scientists think that it may actually be a fully-grown version of another dinosaur called Edmontosaurus rather than its own species!

PRONUNCIATION: an-ah-toh-TIE-tan

DIET: Herbivore

TIME PERIOD: Late Cretaceous

SIZE

SPEED

DEADLY RATING

Oviraptor

The small Oviraptor spent a lot of its time crouching over its nest to look after its eggs and keep them warm. If any predator got too close, Oviraptor could protect them using its very sharp beak that was perfect for crushing things.

PRONUNCIATION: oh-vee-RAP-tor

DIET: Omnivore

TIME PERIOD: Late Cretaceous

SIZE

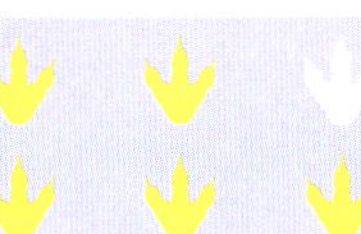

SPEED

DEADLY RATING

Pegomastax

This was a very unusual-looking dinosaur! Covered in spikes like a porcupine, Pegomastax had a short beak like a parrot's, and a pair of fang-like canine teeth. It was very rare for a herbivore to have such big canines! Pegomastax used them to defend itself or to fight other dinosaurs of the same species, rather than to eat meat.

Skull no longer than a pencil!

Blunt beak the perfect shape for picking fruit

Weighed less than a housecat!

PRONUNCIATION: PEG-oh-mas-taks

DIET: Herbivore

TIME PERIOD: Early Jurassic

SIZE

SPEED

DEADLY RATING

Only one fossil has
ever been found!

Heterodontosaurus

Heterodontosaurus is mostly known for having three different kinds of teeth. These teeth allowed it to tear, bite, and grind its food. It also had large cheek pouches to store food in while chewing so that nothing fell out!

Long, flexible tail
Five claws on each front foot

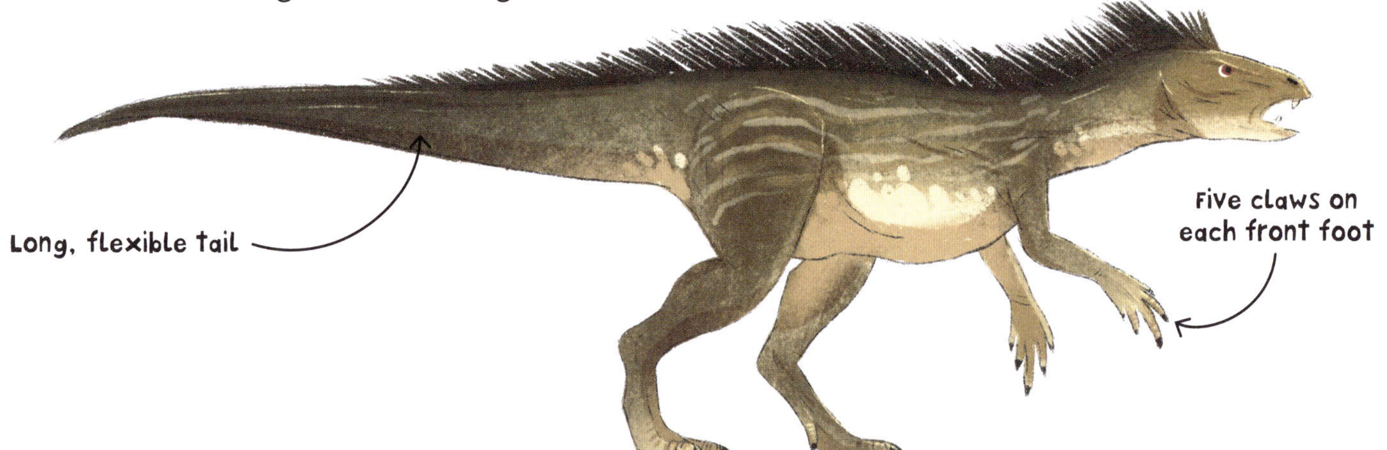

PRONUNCIATION: het-er-oh-DONT-oh-sore-us		**SIZE**	●○○○○
DIET: Herbivore		**SPEED**	●●●○○
TIME PERIOD: Early Jurassic		**DEADLY RATING**	●○○○○

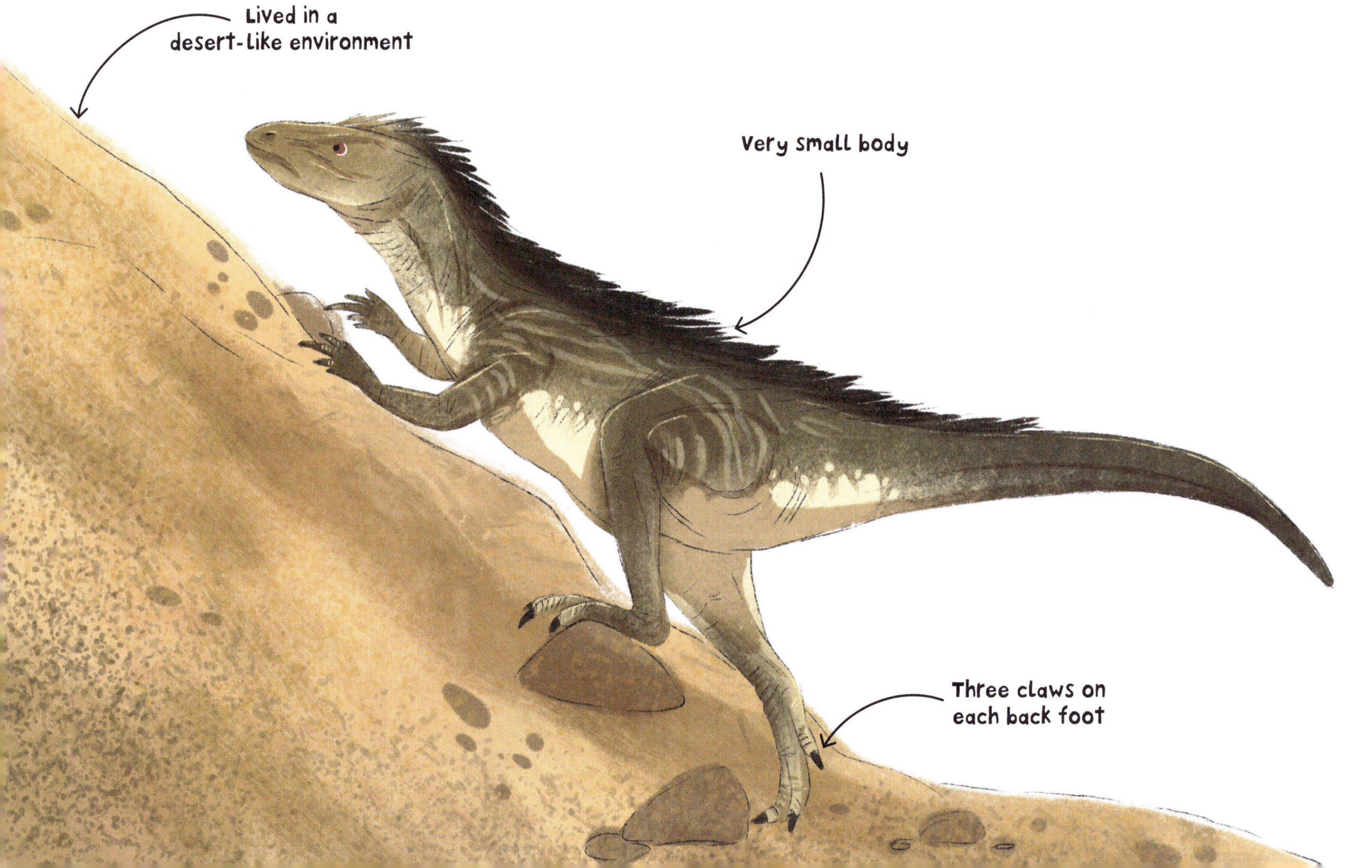
Lived in a desert-like environment
Very small body
Three claws on each back foot

Sinosauropteryx

Sinosauropteryx was the first feathered dinosaur discovered that wasn't related to modern-day birds! It was also the first dinosaur that scientists were able to confidently say what color/colour it was!

PRONUNCIATION: sine-oh-SORE-op-ter-iks	SIZE	
DIET: Carnivore	SPEED	
TIME PERIOD: Early Cretaceous	DEADLY RATING	

Stegosaurus

Stegosaurus is famous for the double row of triangle-shaped plates that ran along its back. These might have had two purposes. They could have been used to protect its spine and back. Alternatively, they could have acted like a radiator, soaking up sunlight to help keep Stegosaurus warm.

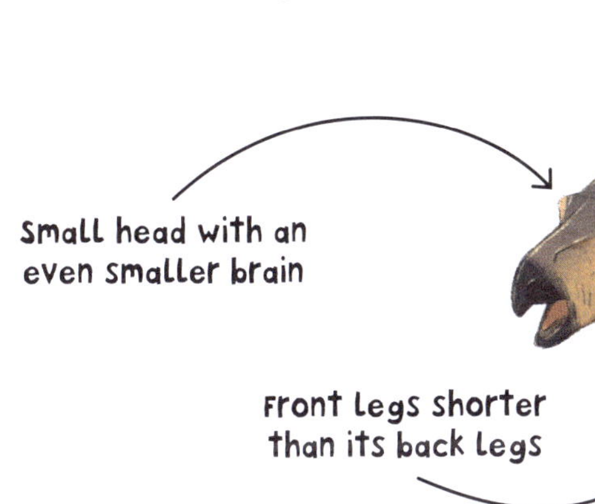

PRONUNCIATION: STEG-oh-SORE-us	SIZE	
DIET: Herbivore	SPEED	
TIME PERIOD: Late Jurassic	DEADLY RATING	

Nothronychus

Nothronychus was a large dinosaur that usually preferred to eat plants. But its family tree shows that this might not have always been the case. Its close relatives were all carnivores, suggesting that Nothronychus changed its diet over time.

PRONUNCIATION: noh-THRON-ee-kus

DIET: Omnivore

TIME PERIOD: Late Cretaceous

SIZE

SPEED

DEADLY RATING

Giraffatitan

Compared to its close relatives like Brachiosaurus (page 46), Giraffatitan had a shorter, thicker tail and a slimmer body. But it still had the classic long neck that made it look like, well, a giraffe!

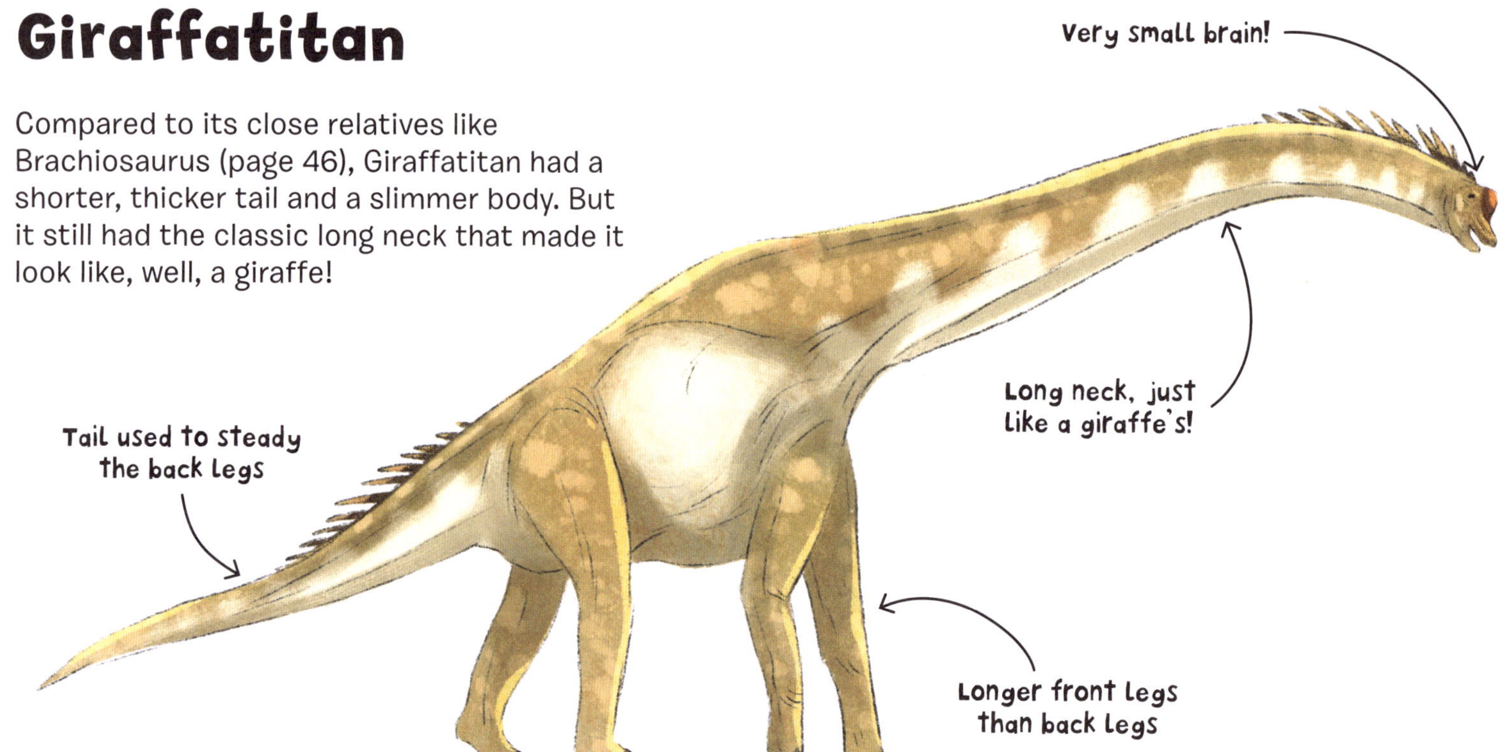

PRONUNCIATION: ji-raf-a-TIE-tan

DIET: Herbivore

TIME PERIOD: Late Jurassic

SIZE

SPEED

DEADLY RATING

Gryposaurus

A giant even compared to other duck-billed dinosaurs, Gryposaurus was the largest dinosaur living in its area. It had over 300 teeth that were perfect for eating almost any plants that it came across.

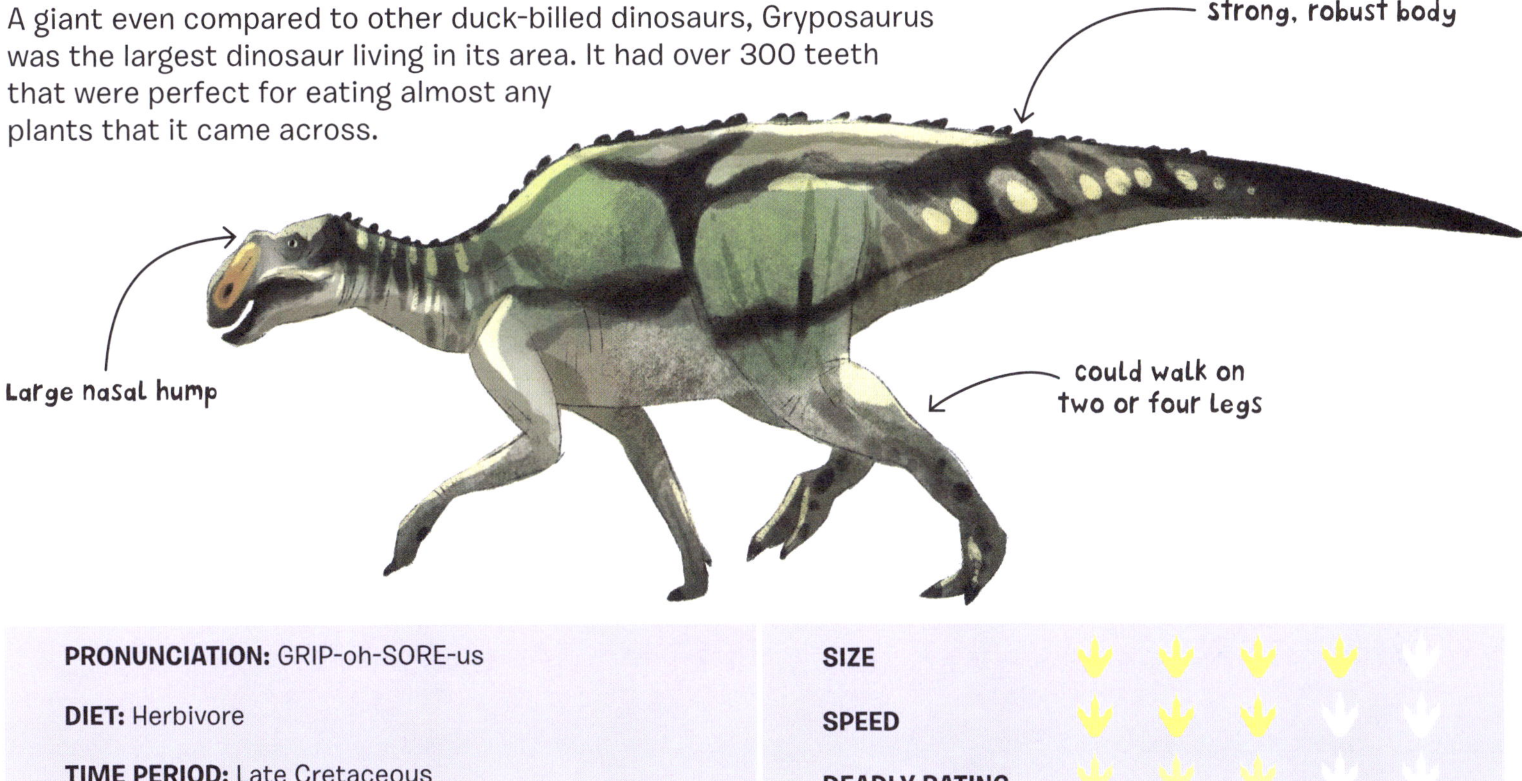

PRONUNCIATION: GRIP-oh-SORE-us

DIET: Herbivore

TIME PERIOD: Late Cretaceous

SIZE

SPEED

DEADLY RATING

Anchiornis

Although it has been called "the earliest bird", Anchiornis was still a dinosaur – the oldest one able to glide, in fact! It shows that some dinosaurs grew feathers and other bird-like features long before true birds developed.

PRONUNCIATION: an-kee-OR-niss

DIET: Carnivore

TIME PERIOD: Late Jurassic

SIZE

SPEED

DEADLY RATING

Corythosaurus

Corythosaurus used the crescent-shaped crest on its head to help produce sounds to communicate with other dinosaurs. It's also possible that the crest was used to control its body temperature or to attract a mate.

PRONUNCIATION: koh-rith-OH-sore-us

DIET: Herbivore

TIME PERIOD: Late Cretaceous

SIZE

SPEED

DEADLY RATING

Rhinorex

Unlike its closest relatives, Rhinorex didn't have a crest on its head. Instead, it had an enormous nose! Unfortunately this didn't mean it had a better sense of smell. Instead, it was used to attract other Rhinorex or to help break up vegetation when eating.

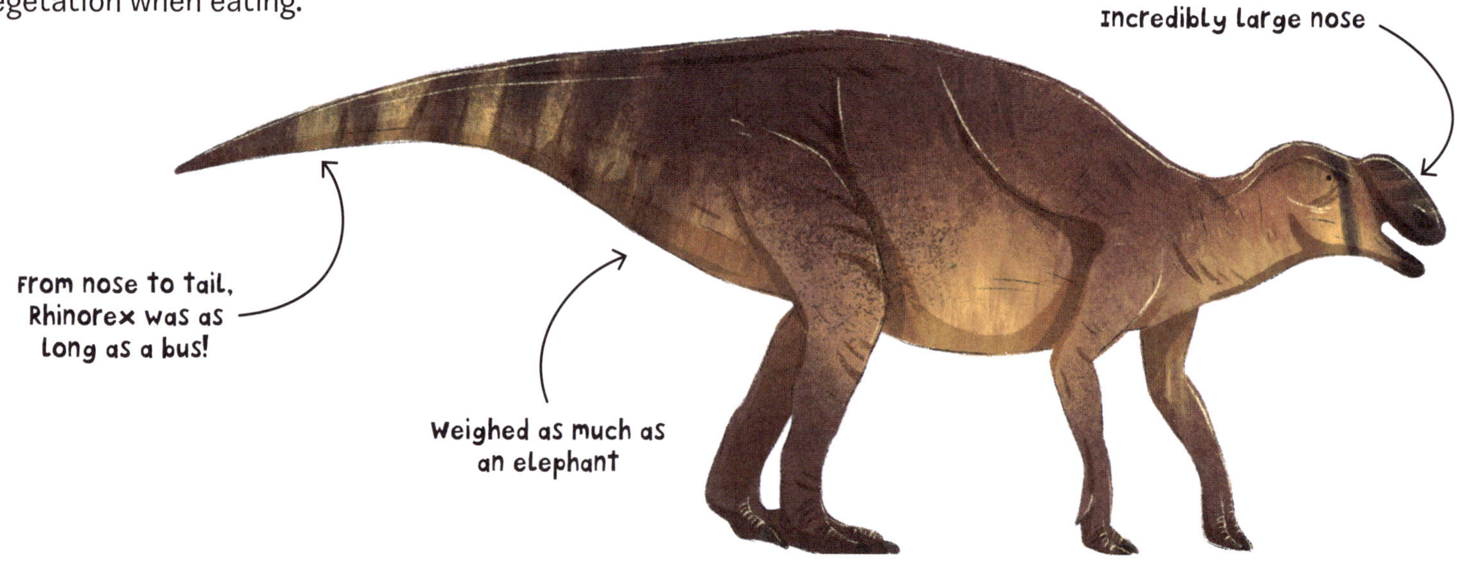

PRONUNCIATION: RY-noh-rex

DIET: Herbivore

TIME PERIOD: Late Cretaceous

SIZE

SPEED

DEADLY RATING

Suzhousaurus

Suzhousaurus was related to the incredibly long-clawed Therizinosaurus (page 29). While not quite as big, Suzhousaurus was still very impressive. It would have used its claws to reach above it and grab branches to eat from.

PRONUNCIATION: su-zoo-SORE-us

DIET: Herbivore

TIME PERIOD: Early Cretaceous

SIZE

SPEED

DEADLY RATING

Concavenator

Concavenator had two tall bones on its spine that gave it an unusual appearance. Whether these bones would have looked like a short, thin sail or like a camel's hump is a mystery to scientists – as is the reason why Concavenator had it in the first place!

PRONUNCIATION: kon-ka-VEN-at-or

DIET: Carnivore

TIME PERIOD: Early Cretaceous

SIZE

SPEED

DEADLY RATING

Mosasaurus

The sleek and streamlined Mosasaurus was among the ocean's deadliest hunters. It used a snake-like movement of its body to push itself through the water in search of prey. It had no predators and wasn't picky about its food – it would eat anything that it came across!

PRONUNCIATION: moh-suh-SORE-us	**SIZE** 4/5
DIET: Carnivore	**SPEED** 3/5
TIME PERIOD: Late Cretaceous	**DEADLY RATING** 4/5

Qianzhousaurus

Qianzhousaurus was a smaller, lighter version of Tyrannosaurus rex (page 13)! It had a distinctive nose that was thinner and longer, giving it the nickname "Pinocchio rex". Because of this, it likely wouldn't have hunted or eaten in the same way as Tyrannosaurus rex, but it was still an intimidating predator!

PRONUNCIATION: key-an-zoo-SORE-us	**SIZE** 3/5
DIET: Carnivore	**SPEED** 3/5
TIME PERIOD: Late Cretaceous	**DEADLY RATING** 3/5

Incisivosaurus

The tiny Incisivosaurus may have been related to very large, fearsome meat-eaters, but besides walking on two legs it had very little in common with them! Incisivosaurus's teeth – including two very large front teeth – suggested that it was a plant-eater instead.

PRONUNCIATION: in-SIZ-oh-voe-SORE-us

DIET: Herbivore or omnivore

TIME PERIOD: Early Cretaceous

SIZE

SPEED

DEADLY RATING

Parasaurolophus

This dinosaur is best known for the long, hollow, backward-curving crest on its head. Scientists believe that Parasaurolophus could blow air through it to create a loud trumpeting sound to communicate with other dinosaurs of the same species.

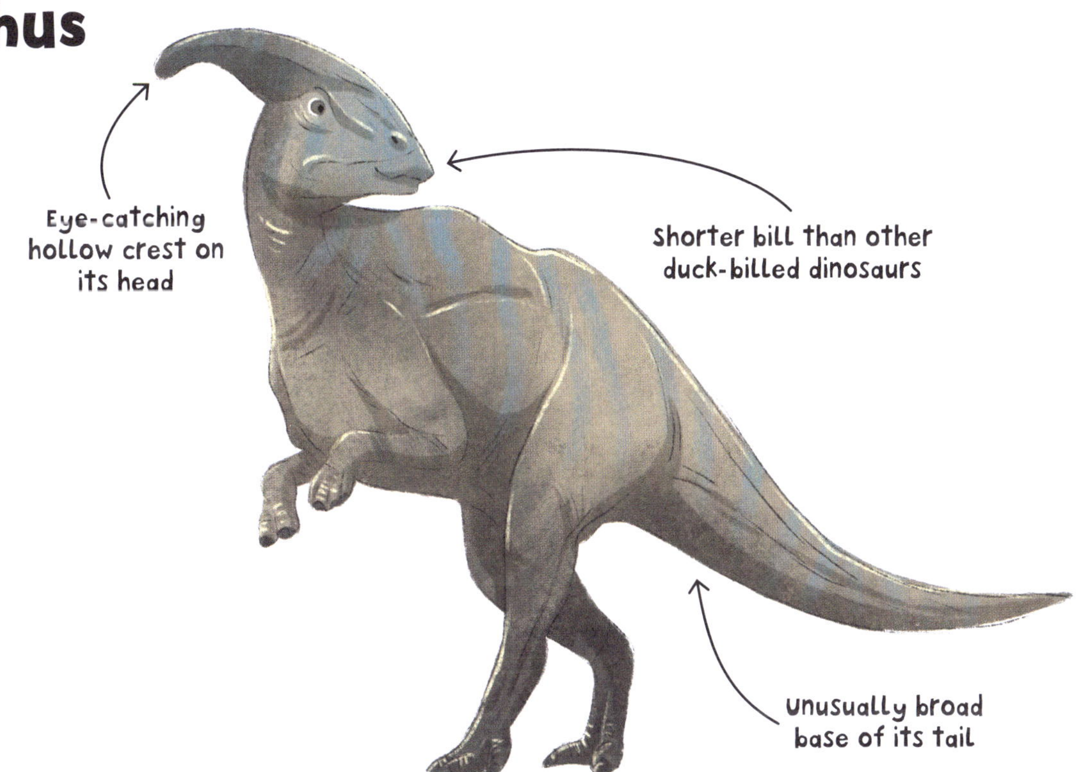

PRONUNCIATION: pa-ra-saw-ROL-off-us

DIET: Herbivore

TIME PERIOD: Late Cretaceous

SIZE

SPEED

DEADLY RATING

GLOSSARY

Agile – the ability to move very quickly and easily.

Armor/armour – a protective outer layer.

Asteroid – small, rocky objects that orbit the Sun.

Carnivore – an animal that only eats meat.

Continent – the huge pieces of land on Earth. For example, Africa and North America are separate continents.

Cretaceous – a period of time that lasted from about 143 to 66 million years ago.

Extinct – a species (see right) of animals with no living members.

Food chain – the order in which different species (see right) eat each other to survive.

Herbivore – an animal that only eats plants.

Hollow – something that has an empty space inside.

Insectivore – an animal that mostly eats insects.

Jurassic – a period of time that lasted from about 201 to 143 million years ago.

Mammals – warm-blooded animals (including humans) that produce milk to feed their young.

Mate – two animals that come together to produce young.

Omnivore – an animal that eats both plants and meat.

Permian – a period of time that lasted from about 299 to 251 million years ago.

Predators – animals that hunt and kill other animals for food.

Prehistoric – the time before humans existed.

Prey – an animal that is hunted by other animals for food.

Reptiles – a group of cold-blooded animals, including snakes, lizards, crocodiles, and some types of dinosaurs.

Sail – a large, flat structure that grows on the backs of certain animals, including some dinosaurs.

Scavengers – an animal that eats animals that are dead instead of hunting for living animals to kill and eat.

Skeleton – the bony frame that supports and protects the body of a person or animal.

Slender – something that is thin and narrow.

Species – a group of living things that share characteristics and features, and can produce young with each other. For example, Stegosaurus and Triceratops are different dinosaur species.

Territory – an area of land that an animal will protect from other animals.

Triassic – a period of time that lasted from about 251 to 201 million years ago.

Unique – something that stands out and is completely different from everything else.

Vegetation - plant life in a particular area.

INDEX

ABOUT THE AUTHORS AND ILLUSTRATOR

Rosie Rowntree is a children's author living in the west of Cornwall. Sharing her love of learning through her writing, she is passionate about sparking curiosity in children as they begin to broaden their horizons and learn about their surroundings - and beyond!

Eliza Jeffery is a children's book author based in Falmouth. She is passionate about helping children explore and enjoy the big world around them. She loves exploring Cornwall, and can often be found reading a book and eating a bowl of mussels by the sea!

Marina Halak is a talented illustrator of children's books from Ukraine. Her stunning illustrations are inspired by her own childhood, children, nature, magical moments and fairy tales. Marina is also the illustrator behind the first two books in the series, *Dogs* and *Cats*.